The Clown in the Belfry

The Clown in the Belfry

Writings on Faith and Fiction

FREDERICK BUECHNER

HarperSanFrancisco
A Division of HarperCollinsPublishers

Credits appear on page 173.

Library of Congress Cataloging-in-Publication Data

Buechner, Frederick
    The clown in the belfry : writings on faith and fiction /
Frederick Buechner. — 1st ed.
        p.   cm.
    ISBN 0-06-061184-7 (alk. paper)
    1. Theology— Miscellanea. 2. Christianity and literature
—Miscellanea. I. Title.
BR85.B8955 1992
252'.051—dc20   91-55414
                                                                  CIP

93 94 95 ❖ HAD 10 9 8 7 6 5 4 3

This edition is printed on acid-free paper that meets the American
National Standards Institute Z39.48 Standard.

for
George Connor

Contents

Introduction

There are fourteen pieces here, six of them sermons which I preached at various times and places over the last five years or so. Two of the sermons ("The Clown in the Belfry" and "Light and Dark") were written for the anniversaries of particular churches—the hundredth anniversary of one, the two hundredth of the other. I considered at first trying to make them more generally relevant somehow but then decided that particularity is what biblical faith is all about and let them stand pretty much as they were. As for the other four, it wasn't till I put them side by side for the first time that I realized how much they all have to do with the Church in general. In one of them I quote from Woody Allen's *Hannah and Her Sisters*, where a character says, "If Jesus came back and saw what was going on in his name, he'd never stop throwing up." As far as I am concerned, that is prophetic truth, and one way or another all four of them deal with what I believe the Church is called by God to become in this befouled and befuddled world and what Jesus originally intended it to be.

The remaining pieces are a real mishmash. There is an address that I delivered at the graduation of my friend Polly Parker from the Westminister School in Connecticut one exceptionally muggy spring day when I can still remember my relief as the sun slowly worked its way beyond a tall elm and gave the speakers' platform some blessed shade at last. There is a piece about Flannery O'Connor which I wrote as an introduction to Jill Baumgaertner's very useful book about her, *A Proper Scaring*, and in which I describe a detour my wife and I once made to Milledgeville, Georgia, where she mostly lived and worked and finally died. "Faith and Fiction" is a lecture I gave one winter at the New York Public Library where I tried to say something about what I think those two expressions of the human spirit have in common and along the way to tell a thing or two about my own involvement with them including a true ghost story. "The Good Book as a Good Book" and "Paul Sends His Love" are both chapters I was asked to write for other people's collections, the first a sort of novelist's eye view of the Bible generally and the second a somewhat closer look at the first of the two letters Saint Paul wrote to the peculiarly troubled and troubling church which he founded among the fleshpots of Corinth. "The Opening of Veins" is a talk that I gave at the Pierpont Morgan Library in New York on the occasion of the annual presentation of the Whiting Writers' awards, and "Adolescence and the Stewardship of Pain" is another that I gave at a symposium at Saint Paul's School.

It is bats that are supposed to be found in belfries, but for a few incandescent moments in 1831 a man named Lyman Woodard was to be found in one that is still higher than any other building in Rupert, Vermont. The event is described in its proper place. Suffice it to say here only that one day he climbed up and stood on his head in that belfry.

Why did he do it? Was he drunk? Was he crazy? Who knows? Who even cares? The point is that it was a gorgeous, clownish, inspired, and inspiring thing to do. It was a radically new way of looking at the mysteries of earth and heaven. It is Saint Paul writing, "We are fools for Christ's sake." It is David dancing naked before the ark. It is the rapturous shenanigans and holy abandon of faith kicking up its heels and considering the lilies of the field from an altogether different vantage. It is what virtually everything in this collection is trying to be about, and hence the title.

The Clown in the Belfry

I

Faith and Fiction

A year or so ago, a friend of mine died. He was an Englishman—witty, elegant, multifaceted. One morning in his sixty-eighth year he simply didn't wake up. It was about as easy a way as he could possibly have done it, but it was not easy for the people he left behind because it gave us no chance to start getting used to the idea beforehand or to say goodbye either in words, if we turned out to be up to it, or in some awkward, unspoken way if we weren't. He died in March, and in May my wife and I were staying with his widow overnight when I had a short dream about him. I dreamed he was standing there in the dark guest room where we were asleep looking very much himself in the navy blue jersey and white slacks he often wore. I told him how much we had missed him and how glad I was to see him again. He acknowledged that somehow. Then I said, "Are you really there, Dudley." I meant was he there in fact, in truth, or was I merely dreaming he was. His answer was that he was really there. "Can you prove it?" I asked him. "Of course," he said. Then he plucked a strand of wool out of his jersey and tossed it to me. I caught it between my thumb and forefinger, and the feel of it was so palpably real that it woke me up. That's all there was to it. It was as if he'd come on purpose to do what he'd done and then left. I told the dream at breakfast the next morning, and I'd hardly finished when my wife spoke. She said that she'd seen the strand on the carpet as she was getting dressed. She was sure it hadn't been there the night before. I rushed upstairs to see for myself, and there it was—a little tangle of navy blue wool.

Another event. I went into a bar in an airport not long ago to fortify myself against my least favorite means of transportation. It was an off hour so I was the only customer and had a choice of the whole row of empty bar stools. On the counter in front of each of them was a holder with a card stuck in it advertising the drink of the day or something like that. I noticed that the one in front of me had a small metal piece on top of the card that wasn't on the others so I took a look at it. It turned out to be a tie-clip that somebody must have stuck there. It had three letters engraved on it, and the letters were C. F. B. Those are my initials.

Lastly this. I was receiving communion in an Episcopal church early one morning. The priest was an acquaintance of mine. I could hear him moving along the rail from person to person as I knelt there waiting my turn. The body of Christ, he said, the bread of Heaven. The body of Christ, the bread of Heaven. When he got to me, he put in another word. The word was my name. "The body of Christ, Freddy, the bread of Heaven."

The dream about my friend may well have been just another dream, and you certainly don't have to invoke the supernatural to account for the thread on the carpet. The tie-clip I find harder to explain away. It seems to me that mathematically speaking the odds against its having not just one or two but all three of my initials on it in the right order must be astronomical, but I suppose that could be just a coincidence too. On the other hand in both cases there is the other possibility too. Far-out or not, I don't see how any open-minded person can a priori deny it, and in a way it is that other possibility, as a possibility, that is at the heart of everything I want to say here.

Maybe my friend really did come to me in my dream and the thread was his sign to me that he had. Maybe it is true that by God's grace the dead are given back their lives again and that the doctrine of the resurrection of the body is not just a doctrine. He couldn't have looked more substantial and less ectoplasmic standing there in the dark, and it was such a crisp, no-nonsense exchange we had with nothing surreal or wispy about it. It was so much like him. As to the tie-clip, it seemed so extraordinary that for a moment I almost refused to believe it had happened at all. I think that's worth marking. Even though I had the thing right there in my hand, my first inclination was to deny it for the simple reason, I suspect, that it was so unsettling to my whole common-sense view of the way the world works that it was easier and less confusing just to shrug it off as a crazy fluke. I think we are all inclined to do that. But maybe it wasn't a fluke. Maybe it was a crazy little peek behind the curtain, a dim little whisper of providence from the wings. I had been expected. I was on schedule. I was taking the right journey at the right time. I was not alone.

What happened at the communion rail was rather different. There was nothing extraordinary about the priest's knowing my name—I knew he knew it—and there was nothing extraordinary about his using it in the service either, I learned later, because it was a practice he not infrequently followed. But its effect upon me was extraordinary. It caught me off guard. It moved me deeply. For the first time in my life perhaps it struck me that when Jesus picked up the bread at his last meal and said, "This is my body which is for you," he was doing it not just in a ritual way for humankind in general but in an unthinkably personal way for every particular man, woman, child who ever existed or someday would exist. Most unthinkable of all, as far as I was concerned, maybe he was doing it for me. At that holiest of feasts, we are known not just by our official names but by the names people use who have known us longest and most intimately. We are welcomed not as the solid citizens that our Sunday best suggests we are but in all our inner tackiness and tatteredness that no one in the world knows better than we each of us know it about ourselves—the bitterness, the phoniness, the confusion, the irritability, the prurience, the half-heartedness. The bread of Heaven, *Freddy*, of all people? Molly? Bill? Ridiculous little What's-her-name? Boring old So-and-so? Extraordinary. It seemed a revelation from on high. Was it?

All that's extraordinary about these three minor events is the fuss I've made about them. Things like that happen every day to everybody. They are a dime a dozen. They mean absolutely nothing.

Or. Things like that are momentary glimpses into a Mystery of such depth, power, beauty, that if we were to see it head-on, we would be annihilated.

If I had to bet my life on one possibility or the other, which one would I bet it on? If you had to bet your life, which one would you bet it on? On *Yes*, there is God in the highest, or, if such language is no longer viable, there is Mystery and Meaning in the deepest? On *No*, there is whatever happens to happen, and it means whatever you choose it to mean, and that is all there is?

We may bet Yes this evening and No tomorrow morning. We may know we are betting or we may not know. We may bet one way with our lips, our minds, our hearts even, and another way with our feet. But we all of us bet, and it's our lives themselves we're betting with in the sense that the betting is what shapes our lives. And we can never be sure we've bet right, of course. The evidence both ways is fragmentary, fragile, ambiguous. A coincidence can be, as somebody has said, God's way of remaining anonymous, or it can be just a coincidence. Is the dream that brings healing and hope just a product of wishful thinking? Or is it a message from another world? Whether we bet Yes or No, it is equally an act of faith.

Religious faith, the Epistle to the Hebrews says in a famous chapter, (Hebrews 11) "is the assurance of things hoped for, the conviction of things not seen." Noah, Abraham, Sarah, and the rest of them, it goes on to say, "all died in faith, not having received what was promised but having seen it and greeted it from afar, and having acknowledged that they were strangers and exiles on the earth. For people [like that] make it clear that they are seeking a homeland."

Faith, therefore, is distinctly different from other aspects of the religious life and not to be confused with them even though we sometimes use the word to mean religious belief in general as in phrases like the Christian faith or the faith of Islam. Faith is different from theology because theology is reasoned, systematic, orderly whereas faith is disorderly, intermittent, and full of surprises. Faith is different from mysticism because mystics in their ecstasy become one with what faith can at most see only from afar. Faith is different from ethics because ethics is primarily concerned not, like faith, with our relationship to God but with our relationship to each other. Faith is closest perhaps to worship because like worship it is essentially a response to God and involves the emotions and the physical senses as well as the mind, but worship is consistent, structured, single-minded and seems to know what it's doing while faith is a stranger and exile on the earth and doesn't know for certain about anything. Faith is homesickness. Faith is a lump in the throat. Faith is less a position *on* than a movement *toward*, less a sure thing than a hunch. Faith is waiting. Faith is journeying through space and through time.

If someone were to come up and ask me to talk about my faith, it is exactly that journey that I would eventually have to talk about—the ups and downs of the years, the dreams, the odd moments, the intuitions. I would have to talk about the occasional sense I have that life is not just a series of events causing other events as haphazardly as a break shot in pool causes the billiard balls to career off in all directions but that life has a plot the way a novel has a plot, that events are somehow or other leading somewhere. Whatever your faith may be or my faith may be, it seems to me inseparable from the story of what has happened to us, and that is why I believe that no literary form is better adapted to the subject than the form of fiction.

Faith and fiction both journey forward in time and space and draw their life from the journey, *are* in fact the journey. Faith and fiction both involve the concrete, the earthen, the particular more than they do the abstract and cerebral. In both, the people you meet along the way, the things that happen, the places—the airport bar, the room where you have your last supper with a friend—count for more than ideas do. Fiction can hold opposites together simultaneously like love and hate, laughter and tears, despair and hope, and so of course does faith which by its very nature both sees and does not see and whose most characteristic utterance, perhaps, is "Lord I believe, help thou my unbelief." Faith and fiction both start once upon a time and are continually changing and growing in mood, intensity, direction. When faith stops changing and growing, it dies on its feet. So does fiction. And they have more in common than that.

They both start with a leap in the dark, for one. How can Noah, Abraham, Sarah, or anyone else know for sure that the promise they die without receiving will ever be kept and that their journey in search of a homeland will ever get them there? How can anybody writing a novel or a story know for sure where it will lead and just how and with what effect it will end or even if it is a story worth telling? Let writers beware who from the start know too much about what they are doing and keep too heavy a hand on the reins. They leave too little room for luck as they tell their stories just the way Abraham and Sarah, if they know too much about what they are doing as they *live* their stories, leave too little room for grace.

The word *fiction* comes from a Latin verb meaning to shape, fashion, feign. That is what fiction does, and in many ways it is what faith does too. You fashion your story, as you fashion your faith, out of the great hodgepodge of your life—the things that have happened to you and the things you have dreamed of happening. They are the raw material of both. Then, if you're a writer like me, you try less to impose a shape on the hodgepodge than to see what shape emerges from it, is hidden in it. You try to sense what direction it is moving in. You listen to it. You avoid forcing your characters to march too steadily to the drumbeat of your artistic purpose but leave them some measure of real freedom to be themselves. If minor characters show signs of becoming major characters, you at least give them a shot at it because in the world of fiction it may take many pages before you find out who the major characters really are just as in the real world it may take you many years to find out that the stranger you talked to for half an hour once in a railway station may have done more to point you to where your true homeland lies than your closest friend or your psychiatrist.

As a writer I use such craft as I have at my command, of course. I figure out what scenes to put in and, just as important, what scenes to leave out. I decide when to use dialogue and spend hours trying to make it sound like human beings talking to each other instead of just me talking to myself. I labor to find the right tone of voice to tell my story in, which is to say the right style, ultimately the right word, which is the most demanding part of it all—sentence after sentence, page after page, looking for the word that has freshness and power and life in it. But I try not to let my own voice be the dominant one. The limitation of the great stylists, of course—

of a James, say, or a Hemingway—is that it is their voices you remember long after you have forgotten the voices of any of their characters. "Be still and know that I am God," is the advice of the Psalmist, and I've always taken it to be good literary advice too. Be still the way Tolstoy is still, or Anthony Trollope is still, so your characters can speak for themselves and come alive in their own way.

In faith and fiction both you *fashion* out of the raw stuff of your experience. If you want to remain open to the luck and grace of things anyway, you *shape* that stuff in the sense less of imposing a shape on it than of discovering the shape. And in both you *feign*—feigning as imagining, as making visible images for invisible things. Fiction can't be true the way a photograph is true, but at its best it can feign truth the way a good portrait does, inward and invisible truth. Fiction at its best can be true to the experience of being a human in this world, and the fiction you write depends, needless to say, on the part of that experience you choose. The part that has always most interested me is best illustrated by such incidents as the three I described at the outset. The moment that unaccountably brings tears to your eyes; that takes you by crazy surprise; that sends a shiver down your spine; that haunts you with what is just possibly a glimpse of something far beyond or deep within itself. That is the part of the human experience I choose to write about in my fiction. It is the part I am most concerned to feign, that is make images for. In that sense I can live with the label of religious novelist. In any other sense, it is a label that makes my flesh crawl.

I lean over backwards not to preach or propagandize in my fiction. I don't dream up plots and characters to illustrate some homiletic message. I am not bent on driving home some theological point. I am simply trying to conjure up stories in which people are touched with what may or may not be the presence of God in their lives as I believe we all of us are even though we might sooner be shot dead than use that kind of language to describe it. In my own experience, the ways God appears in our lives are elusive and ambiguous always. There is always room for doubt in order, perhaps, that there will always be room to breathe. There is so much in life that hides God and denies the very possibility of God that there are times when it is hard not to deny God altogether. Yet it is possible to have faith nonetheless. Faith *is* that Nonetheless. That is the experience I am trying to be true to in the same way that other novelists try to be true to the experience of being a woman, say, or an infantryman in the Second World War. In all of them, there is perhaps nothing more crucial than honesty.

If you are going to be a religious novelist, you have got to be honest not just about the times that glimmer with God's presence but also about the ones that are dark with his absence because needless to say you have had your dark times like everybody else. Terrible things happen in the four novels (*Lion Country, Open Heart, Love Feast,* and *Treasure Hunt*) I wrote about Leo Bebb. In a drunken fit, Bebb's wife, Lucille, kills her own baby, and when Bebb tells her long afterwards that she has been washed clean in the blood of the Lamb, she answers him by saying, "Bebb, the only thing I've been washed in is the shit of the horse," and dies a suicide. Poor Brownie, reeking of after-shave, decides in the end that his rose-colored faith in the goodness of things is as false as his china choppers and loses it. Miriam Parr dies of cancer wondering if she is "going someplace," as she puts it, or "just out like a match." The narrator is a rather feckless, rootless young man named Antonio Parr, who starts out in the first book with no sense of commitment to anything or anybody but who, through his relationship with Leo Bebb, gradually comes alive to at least the possibility of something like religious faith. He has learned to listen for God in the things that happen to him anyway, just in case there happens to be a God to listen for. Maybe all he can hear, he says, is "Time's winged chariot hurrying near." Or, if there is more to it than that, the most he can say of it constitutes the passage with which the last of the four novels ends in which he uses the Lone Ranger as an image for Christ. "To be honest, I must say that on occasion I hear something else too—not the thundering of distant hoofs, maybe, or *Hi-yo, Silver. Away!* echoing across the lonely sage, but the faint chunk-chunk of my own moccasin heart, of the Tonto afoot in the dusk of me somewhere who, not because he ought to but because he can't help himself, whispers *Kemo Sabe* every once in a while to what may or may not be only a silvery trick of the failing light."*

Terrible things as well as wonderful things happen in those books, but it's not so much that I have to cook them up in order to give a balanced view of the way life is as it is that they have a way of happening as much on their own in the fictional world as in the real world. If you're preaching or otherwise grinding an axe, you let happen, of course, only the things you want to have happen; but insofar as fiction, like faith, is a journey not only forward in space and time

---

*Frederick Buechner, *The Book of Bebb* (New York: Atheneum, 1979; papercover, San Francisco: HarperCollins, 1990), p. 530.

but a journey inward, it is full of surprises. Even the wonderful things—the things that religious writers in the propagandist sense would presumably orchestrate and control most of all—tend at their best to come as a surprise, and that is what is most wonderful about them. In the case of the Bebb books again, for instance, I was well along into *Lion Country*, the first of them, before I came to the surprising conclusion that Bebb himself was, wonderfully, a saint.

Imagine setting out consciously to write a novel about a saint. How could you avoid falling flat on your face? Nothing is harder to make real than holiness. Certainly nothing is harder to make appealing and attractive. The danger, I suppose, is that you start out with the idea that sainthood is something people achieve, that you get to be holy more or less the way you get to be an Eagle Scout. To create a saint from that point of view would be to end up with something on the order of Little Nell.

The truth, of course, is that holiness is not a human quality like virtue. If there is such a thing at all, holiness is Godness and as such is not something people do but something God does in them if there is such a thing as God. It is something God seems especially apt to do in people who are not virtuous at all, at least not to start with. Think of Francis of Assisi or Mary Magdalene. Quite the contrary. If you're too virtuous, the chances are you think you are a saint already under your own steam, and therefore the real thing can never happen to you. Leo Bebb was not an Eagle Scout. He ran a religious diploma mill and ordained people through the mail for a fee. He did five years in the pen on a charge of indecent exposure involving children. He had a child by the wife of his twin brother. But he was a risk-taker. He was as round and fat and as full of bounce as a rubber ball. He was without pretense. He was good company. Above all else, he was extraordinarily alive—so much so for me anyway that when I was writing about him I could hardly wait to get back to my study every morning. That's when I began not only to see that he was a saint but to see also what a saint is.

A saint is a life-giver. I hadn't known that before. A saint is a human being with the same sorts of hang-ups and abysses as the rest of us, but if a saint touches your life, you become alive in a new way. Even aimless, involuted Antonio Parr came more alive through knowing Bebb though at first he was out to expose him as a charlatan. So did the theosophist Gertrude Conover, Bebb's blue-haired octogenarian paramour. More extraordinary yet, I came more alive myself. I am a bookish, private sort of man, but in my old age I find myself doing and saying all sorts of outrageous things which, before Bebb came into my life and my fiction, I would have never even considered. I didn't think Bebb up at all the way he finally emerged as a character—sometimes I wonder if he was the one who thought me up. I had another kind of character in mind entirely when I started. In his tight-fitting raincoat and Tyrolean hat, he simply turned out to be the person he was in the journey of writing those books. I didn't expect him. I didn't deserve him. He came making no conditions. There were no strings attached. He was a free gift.

That is also what grace is—to use the religious word for it. Grace is God in his givenness. Faith is not *sui generis*. It is a response to the givenness of grace. Faith is given a glimpse of *something*, however dimly. Men and women of faith know they are strangers and exiles on the earth because somehow and somewhere along the line they have been given a glimpse of home. Maybe the little tangle of navy blue wool on the carpet was grace, even if it could be proved that it had only come from my own sweater. By grace we see what we see. To have faith is to respond to what we see by longing for it the rest of our days; by trying to live up to it and toward it through all the wonderful and terrible things; by breathing it in like air and growing strong on it; by looking to see it again and see it better. To lose faith is to stop looking. To lose faith is to decide, like Brownie, that all you ever saw from afar was your own best dreams.

The whole idea of the Muse is another way of speaking of this same matter of course, the goddess who inspires. And the word *in-spiration* itself as a *breathing into* is another. In fiction as in faith something from outside ourselves is breathed into us if we're lucky, if we're open enough to inhale it. I think writers of religious fiction especially have to stay open in that way. They've got to play their hunches more and take risks more. They shouldn't try to keep too tight a rein on what they're doing. They should be willing to be less professional and literary and more eccentric, antic, disheveled— less like John Updike or Walker Percy, maybe, and more like Kurt Vonnegut, or Peter de Vries, or G. K. Chesterton. In the stories of Flannery O'Connor, for instance, I have a sense of the author herself being caught off guard by a flash of insight here, a stab of feeling there. She is making discoveries about holy things and human things in a way that I think would never have been possible if she had known too well where she was going and how she was going to get there; and as her readers we share in the freshness and wonder of her surprise. I suppose *The Brothers Karamazov* would be the classic example of what I'm talking about—that great seething bouillabaisse of a book. It is digressive and sprawling, with many too many characters in it and much too long, and yet it is a book which, just because Dostoevsky leaves room in it for whatever comes up to enter, is entered here and there by maybe no less than the Holy Spirit itself, thereby becoming, as far as I am concerned, what at its best a religious novel can be—that is to say a novel less *about* the religious experience than a novel the reading of which itself *is* a religious experience—of God both in his subterranean presence and in his appalling absence.

Is it the Holy Spirit? Is it the Muse? Is it just a lucky break? Who dares say without crossing the fingers. But as in the journey of faith it is possible every once and a while to be better than you are—"Do you not know that . . . God's spirit dwells within you?" Paul asks—in the journey of fiction-making it is possible to write more than you know. Bebb was a saint—a kind of saint anyway—and when I finally finished with him, or he with me, I found that it was very hard to write a novel about any other kind of person. I tried a fifteenth-century alchemist, a twentieth-century woman novelist, a dishwasher in a New England restaurant, an old lady in a nursing home, and one by one they failed to come to life for me. They were all in their own ways too much like me, I suppose, and after so many years I have come to be a little tired of me. And too many other authors were writing novels about people like that, many of them better than I could do it, so why add to the number? Then I realized that more even than those reasons, the basic reason that none of them worked for me was that, after Bebb, only saints really interest me as a writer. There is so much life in them. They are so in touch with, so transparent to, the mystery of things that you never know what to expect from them. Anything is possible for a saint. They won't stay put or be led around by the nose no matter how hard you try. And then entirely by accident one day—or by grace, or by luck—I came across an historical saint whom I'd never heard of before even by name. He was born in England in the year 1065 and died there in the year 1170. His name was Godric.

If, like me, you don't happen to be a saint yourself, I don't know how you write about one without being given something from somewhere. That is especially true if you try, as I did, to make the saint himself your narrator so that you have his whole interior life on your hands as well as his career. Add to that, Godric was a man who was born close to a thousand years ago—lived in a different world, spoke a different language, saw things in a different way. I did some research, needless to say—not of the thoroughgoing sort that I assume a real historical novelist undertakes because it wasn't primarily the historical period that I was interested in but, rather, Godric himself. Nonetheless I read enough to give myself some idea of roughly what was going on in Europe at the time, especially in England. Largely through the ineffable *Dictionary of National Biography*, I found out what I could about such historical figures who played parts in Godric's life as Abbot Ailred of Rievaulx Abbey and Ranulf Flambard, Bishop of Durham and former chancellor to William the Second. I tried with meager success to find out what Rome and Jerusalem looked like when Godric made his pilgrimages there. I dug a little into the First Crusade because Godric was briefly involved with it apparently. The principal source on Godric himself is a contemporary biography written by a monk known as Reginald of Durham, who knew him and who figures as a character in the novel. The book has never been translated from medieval Latin, and in that regard something rather remarkable happened comparable to the discovery of the tie-clip with my initials on it. My own Latin came to an end with Caesar's *Commentaries* some fifty years ago so the best I could do was look up promising references in the English index and then try to get at least the gist of them with the help of a dictionary. Then, just as I was getting started on that, one of my daughters, who was off at boarding school, phoned to ask if she could bring some friends home for the weekend, and one of the friends turned out to be chairman of the school's classics department. I suppose he was the only person within a radius of a hundred miles or more who could have done the job, and both evenings he was with us he gave me sight translations of the passages I was after.

But I am talking about something even odder than that and more precious. I am talking about how, by something like grace, you are given every once in a while to be better than you are and to write more than you know. Less because of the research I did than in spite of it, Godric came alive for me—that is what I was given: the way he thought, the way he spoke, the humanness of him, the holiness of him. I don't believe any writer can do that just by taking thought and effort and using the customary tools of the craft. Something else has to happen more mysterious than that. Godric not only came alive for me, but he came speaking words that had a life and a twist to them that I can't feel entirely responsible for. I don't want to make it sound spookier than it was. I was the one who wrote his words, of course. In some sense I invented them, dredged them up out of some sub-basement of who I am. But the words were more like him than they were like me, and without him I feel certain I could never have found them and written them.

Year after year as a hermit in the north of England, the old man used to chasten his flesh in all seasons by bathing in the river Wear a few miles out of Durham. When he got too feeble to do that, he had a servant dig a hole in the chapel he had built for the Virgin Mary and fill it with water from the river so he could still bathe in it there. Here is a passage from the novel where he describes what it was like both to bathe in the river in midwinter and, later, to bathe in the little pool of it in the chapel.

First there's the fiery sting of cold that almost stops my breath, the aching torment in my limbs. I think I may go mad, my wits so outraged that they seek to flee my skull like rats a ship that's going down. I puff. I gasp. Then inch by inch a blessed numbness comes. I have no legs, no arms. My very heart grows still. These floating hands are not my hands. This ancient flesh I wear is rags for all I feel of it.

"Praise, praise!" I croak. Praise God for all that's holy, cold, and dark. Praise him for all we lose, for all the river of the years bears off. Praise him for stillness in the wake of pain. Praise him for emptiness. And as you race to spill into the sea, praise him yourself, old Wear. Praise him for dying and the peace of death.

In the little church I built of wood for Mary, I hollowed out a place for him. Perkin brings him by the pail and pours him in. Now that I can hardly walk, I crawl to meet him there. He takes me in his chilly lap to wash me of my sins. Or I kneel down beside him till within his depths I see a star.

Sometimes this star is still. Sometimes she dances. She is Mary's star. Within that little pool of Wear she winks at me. I wink at her. The secret that we share I cannot tell in full. But this much I will tell. What's lost is nothing to what's found, and all the death that ever was, set next to life, would scarcely fill a cup. *

Feigning is part of it. Imagining, image-making. Reaching deep. But it feels like more than that. Godric told me things I didn't know. He revealed something of himself to me and something of the distant past. He also revealed something of myself to me and something of the not so distant future. I will grow old. I will die. I think it was through his eyes that I first saw beyond the inevitability of it to the mercy of it. "All's lost. All's found." I have faith that that is true, or someday will turn out to be true, but on the old saint's lips the words have a ring of certitude and benediction from which I draw courage as I think I could not from any words merely of my own.

Is that why we write, people like me—to keep our courage up? Are novels such as mine a kind of whistling in the dark? I think so. To whistle in the dark is more than just to try to *convince* yourself that dark is not all there is. It is also to *remind* yourself that dark is not all there is or the end of all there is because even in the dark there is hope. Even in the dark you have the power to whistle, and sometimes that

---

*Frederick Buechner, *Godric* (New York: Atheneum, 1980; papercover, San Francisco: Harper & Row, 1983), pp. 95–96.

seems more than just your own power because it is powerful enough to hold the dark back. The tunes you whistle in the dark are the images you make of that hope, that power. They are the books you write.

In just the same way faith could be called a kind of whistling in the dark too, of course. The living out of faith. The writing out of fiction. In both you shape, you fashion, you feign. Maybe what they have most richly in common is a way of paying attention. Page by page, chapter by chapter, the story unfolds. Day by day, year by year, your own story unfolds, your life's story. Things happen. People come and go. The scene shifts. Time runs by, runs out. Maybe it is all utterly meaningless. Maybe it is all unutterably meaningful. If you want to know which, pay attention. What it means to be truly human in a world that half the time we are in love with and half the time scares the hell out of us—any fiction that helps us pay attention to that is as far as I am concerned religious fiction.

The unexpected sound of your name on somebody's lips. The good dream. The odd coincidence. The moment that brings tears to your eyes. The person who brings life to your life. Maybe even the smallest events hold the greatest clues. If it is God we are looking for, as I suspect we all of us are even if we don't think of it that way and wouldn't use such language on a bet, maybe the reason we haven't found him is that we are not looking in the right places.

Pay attention. As a summation of all that I have had to say as a writer, I would settle for that. And as a talisman or motto for that journey in search of a homeland, which is what faith is, I would settle for that too.

Bibliography

"Faith and Fiction" was originally given as one of a series of talks conceived and produced by Book-of-the-Month-Club, Inc., and eventually published in 1988 by Houghton Mifflin as *Spiritual Quests*. All the participating authors, including myself, were asked to provide bibliographies of the religious writings that had been particularly helpful to them. In addition to listing the books themselves, I tried to say something about what I found and continue to find in each of them.

Graham Greene's *The Power and the Glory*. I don't know that there is any other single novel that has influenced me as much or moved me as often. The whiskey priest, seedy and feckless, is also a kind of saint because—who knows why?—God has chosen to use him that way. Virtually every life he touches is brought to life a little more though he himself is quite unaware of it. That is what saints are: life-givers. I never knew that before.

King Lear is, as far as I am concerned, not only Shakespeare's greatest play but also one of the greatest of all preachments. What it is about, in its depths, is the question of God, and I know of no work that explores it with such anguished honesty and profundity.

Dostoevsky's *The Brothers Karamazov* is another of my extra-canonical Scriptures. Everything you want to know about anything is in it, including one of the most eloquent affirmations of religious faith I am aware of and one of the most devastating attacks on it.

I read G. K. Chesterton's *The Man Who Was Thursday* first when I was about fourteen and have been rereading it ever since. It is a myth both richly comic and nightmarish, and the scene at the end, where you (and Chesterton too) discover at last who Sunday really is, is a theophany second in power only to the last four chapters of the Book of Job.

Which Oz book will I choose? *The Wizard*, which is about a little man who is both a humbug and the greatest wizard of them all, not to mention also about you and me as we bumble along in search of what comes alive in us through seeking it? *Rinkitink*, which is about a fat king, a truculent goat, and three pearls whose magic I suspect we might all be able to work if we only had our heads screwed on right? To my way of thinking, almost any will do. I lived a year in Oz (1932) and have been homesick for it ever since. In the realm of fairy tales, try also E. Nesbit's masterpiece, *The Enchanted Castle*, and the three greatest of C. S. Lewis's Narnia books: *The Magician's Nephew*, *The Lion, the Witch, and the Wardrobe*, and *The Last Battle* read in that order. If you want to understand the secret of the fairy tale as "*evangelium*, giving a fleeting glimpse of Joy, Joy beyond the walls of the world, poignant as grief," read J. R. R. Tolkien's essay "On Fairy-Stories" in his *Tree and Leaf* (in *The Tolkien Reader*, Ballantine Books).

E. M. Forster's *Aspects of the Novel*, particularly the chapter on prophecy, is invaluable for the sense it gives of what religious fiction can be at its best. His paragraphs on the difference, in that genre, between Dostoevsky and George Eliot teach a lesson that no one who tries a hand at it should ever forget.

There is no poet I return to more often than Gerard Manley Hopkins. No other *sees* so eye-achingly well, the Eliot Porter of the Victorians, or stirs the blood with so haunting and holy a ragtime. The desolations of the sonnets of 1885, the exaltations of "The Windhover," "St. Alphonsus Rodriguez," "The Starlight Night," the wrenched and compacted immensities of "The Wreck of the *Deutschland*" are surely among the most deep-drawn utterances of Christian experience.

As to Christianity in itself, David Read's short *The Christian Faith* (Scribner's) sets it forth, doctrine by doctrine, as succinctly yet never superficially as anything comparable I have come on since. In two collections of Paul Tillich's brief sermons—*The Shaking of the Foundations* and *The New Being*—this giant among twentieth-century theologians takes crucial religious words like *sin* and *salvation* and shows that they are not the threadbare banalities they are often taken for (and presented as) but are instead rich with meaning about the human condition and the experience of the divine. Andres Nygren in his *Agape and Eros* distinguishes between the downward reaching gift-love of God and the upward-reaching need-love of man and then traces the course of Church history as one or the other of them has predominated down through the centuries. Lastly, as one who would be a Mahayana Buddhist if he were not a Christian, I recommend Heinrich Zimmer's *Philosophies of India* as a fascinating overview of Indian thinking generally. His chapter on "The Way of the Bodhisattva" is a particularly vivid and eloquent evocation of those great savior figures whose dispassionate love for saints and sinners alike approaches the New Testament concept of *agape* and whose decision to postpone indefinitely their entrance into the bliss of Nirvana in order to return again and again into a world of suffering until the last one of us has been enlightened is a fanciful and moving foreshadowing, seismic with laughter, of the Incarnation.

2

The Good Book as a Good Book

As an occasional writer of novels, I have always thought that
the most appealing aspect of the form is that it allows you
to do anything you can get away with. I think of *Moby Dick*
with its endless excursions into the minutiae of whaledom,
or *Ulysses, Tristram Shandy, The Countesse of Pembroke's Arcadia*
with their endless excursions into everything else. Or I think
of the later novels of Henry James—*The Golden Bowl*, for
instance—where the star of the show is not the story it tells
or the characters it tells about but the sheer madness of the
style, or of Anthony Trollope's *The Warden*, which has virtually no style at all but like a clear window pane allows you to
watch the dance old Septimus Harding's delicate conscience
leads him without the sound of anyone's voice in your ears
except his own. The Bible is not a novel, needless to say, but
like a novel there is almost nothing it does not attempt and
by and large not much that it fails to get away with. In that
sense it is not only the Good Book but a book which, except
for a few notorious *longueurs*, is a remarkably good one. You
might better say that it is not really a book at all but a
library of some sixty-six of them written over the course of

centuries by Heaven only knows whom, or for how many divergent purposes, or from how many variegated points of view, yet in some sense it manages to be one book even so. Something holds it together. When we think of it, we think of it somehow as a whole.

A novelist, for example, might well envy the way the opening chapters of Genesis set the stage for everything that is to follow and foreshadow all the great biblical themes. Creation is one of them. "In the beginning God *created,*" the opening words proclaim, and from there right on to the Book of Revelation it is proclaimed again and again. More almost than anything else he does, as the Bible depicts him, God makes things. He makes the world in all its splendor, and the psalms never stop stammering out their wonder at it— "Praise him, sun and moon, praise him all you shining stars! Praise him, you highest heavens, and all you waters above the heavens! Let them praise the name of the Lord! For he commanded and they were created" (Psalm 148:3–5).

When God presents his credentials to Job in what is perhaps the greatest of all his arias, it is the creation that he himself points to—the springs of the sea and the storehouses of the snow are his, he says; the young lions crouch in their dens, the ostrich waves her proud wings, Behemoth makes the deep boil like a pot, because with his fathomless ingenuity he made them that way. Men and women he made too, of course, and perhaps because he loved them most, perhaps to make it up to them for all the trouble he saw in store for them because they were so bad at loving him back, he made them a little like himself. Even after their fall and the terrible sentence pronounced upon them, "he made for Adam and for his wife garments of skins and clothed them," Genesis says

(3:11), and in a way the entire remainder of the Bible is about how history itself is the record of the Creator's endless efforts to restore his creation to himself, to clothe it again in the glory for which he created it in the first place.

He also made a people, Israel, to be a blessing to all peoples. He raised up prophets to bring them to heel when they strayed. Somewhat reluctantly he anointed kings to rule over them. When his people abandoned him to go wantoning after other gods, he made a people within a people out of the faithful few who were left—"brought forth a shoot out of the stump of Jesse"—and when those few fell away also, he came down finally to making one single person, a second Adam, who was like no other because "in him all the fullness of God was pleased to dwell," as Saint Paul tried to explain the mystery of it to the Colossians (Colossians 1:19). Finally, having funneled down to that single person, the whole vast creative process starts funneling out again through the twelve disciples to, little by little, a new people altogether—a new Israel, the Church—which, ragged and inadequate as it must always be in its humanness, in its holiness is yet another garment that the Creator has fashioned for the sheltering of the creation which for better or worse, as Genesis suggests, he can never stop loving because he made it and it is his. Being what it is, the human race will go on failing till the end of time, but even at the end of time God is there again, as John finally tells it. "Behold, I make all things new!" he calls forth, and while the words are still on his lips, the new Jerusalem he has created comes down out of heaven like a bride.

Creation is perhaps the greatest of the themes adumbrated in the opening chapters of this extraordinary book of books, but of course all the other great themes are implicit in those chapters too. The old covenant of law grows out of God's telling Adam and Eve that all Eden is theirs if only they will not eat of that one fatal tree; and the whole tragic history of Israel, not to mention of the rest of us, stems from their eating it anyway; and out of those garments of skins as emblematic of the love that will not let them go grows the new covenant of grace where nothing is asked of them except that they allow themselves to be clothed. As Saint Paul understood it, in the face of Adam, who went wrong, are already faintly visible the features of Jesus, who went right, was right, lived and died to make all things finally right and whole. "Happy families are all alike; every unhappy family is unhappy in its own way," is how Tolstoy wonderfully and unforgettably sets the stage for all eight hundred pages or more of the *Anna Karenina* to come. The opening pages of Genesis do much the same for the whole great library that it unlocks.

Genesis sets the stage for the drama, and then of course there is the cast of characters. Who can count their number? Who can describe their variety?—patriarchs and judges, kings and courtesans, peasants and priests; in short, men and women of every possible sort, heroes and scoundrels and some, like ourselves, who from time to time manage to be something of both. The central character, of course—the one who dominates everything and around whom all the others revolve—is God himself. The Bible is God's book. It is as unimaginable without him as *Moby Dick* would be without the great white whale, yet like the great white whale, he is scarcely to be seen. He appears briefly walking in Eden in the cool of the day, but there is no description of him there, nor is there one anywhere else in all those thousand pages and more that come later. Such is his holiness that to look upon him is death, and the commandment to make no graven image of him or of anything else in the heaven above or the earth beneath that might be supposed to be like him is basic to the faith of Israel. When Moses is allowed to take refuge in the cleft of a rock so that he may see his glory passing by, God tells him, "You shall see my back; but my face shall not be seen" (Exodus 33:18), and when Moses comes down from talking with God on Mount Sinai, his own face shines with such an unearthly light that the people are afraid to come near him until he puts on a veil (Exodus 34:29). God is not to be seen in this book that is his except as he is reflected in the faces and lives of people who have encountered him, and the whole New Testament grows out of the experience of those who, like Saint Paul, encountered "the glory of God in the face of Christ" (2 Corinthians 4:6).

God is not to be seen in space because in space he is not seeable any more than in *La Comédie Humaine* Balzac is seeable. But he can be *heard*. God's words can be heard because words move forward not through space but through time, and although time cannot be inhabited by eternity, it can be impinged upon by eternity the way the horizontal can be impinged upon by the vertical. God is known in the Bible as he speaks—speaks to and through the prophets and patriarchs, the priests and poets, speaks through the mighty acts he works both in the history of Israel and in the small histories of men and women when their ears and lives are in some measure attuned to him, or sometimes even when they are not. The Bible is the Word of God—the word about God and God's word about himself—and it is also the endless words of God, the unanticipatable and elusive self-disclosures of God to countless numbers of people through the medium of what in Hebrew is called *dabhar*, which means both *word* and *deed*—the word that is also a deed because it makes things happen, and the deed that is also a word because, through it, is revealed meaning.

How remote, inaccessible, amorphous all this makes God sound, yet as the Bible depicts him, he is anything but that. God is now wrathful, now loving. He is jealous. He laughs. He cries out like a woman in labor. He is Abraham's friend. He destroys cities. He speaks in the still, small voice that Elijah heard and answers Moses in thunder. He makes himself known to thousands through the cataclysms of history and hides himself from thousands of others, hides himself—inexplicably, horrifyingly—even from Christ in his dying. It is God himself who says what he ultimately is, the only one who can do it. "I the Lord your God am holy," he says to Moses (Leviticus 19:2), which is another way of saying, "I am who I am." Mystery, power, righteousness, love even—all the words that we use to describe him are in the end as crude as the behavior the Bible ascribes to him. He is none of them. He is all of them. He is who he is experienced to be by Eve, by Rachel, by Ahab, by Hannah, by Bathsheba, by Judas. He is who he is experienced to be by each one of us. He is holy. He is God.

As to the Eves and Hannahs, the Judases and Ahabs themselves—the rest of the cast—we wish we could know what they looked liked, but for the most part the Bible is interested much less in seeing than in hearing and tells us as little about these matters as it does in the case of God. We are told that David was a handsome redhead with beautiful eyes. We are told that Joseph had a coat that was the envy of his brothers, that the bride in Solomon's song had breasts like two fawns, twins of a gazelle, that feed among the lilies. We are told that when Jesus fell asleep in the stern of the boat, he had a pillow under his head, and that Paul was weak in his bodily presence and his speech of no account. But how much we would give to see more—especially when it comes to the leading characters, the ones who not only loomed large in their time but have continued to do so ever since. Abraham and Sarah for instance. Just one glimpse of their ancient, sand-blasted faces when the angel told them they were to have a child at last would be as precious almost as to them the child was. Or the way Moses looked as he stood on Mount Pisgah letting his gaze wander from the lands of Dan and Naphtali in the north to the Negeb and the Jordan valley in the south knowing that he would not live to set foot on any of it. Or Solomon in all his glory, or Mary when the angel came upon her with his troubling word. We are allowed to see that pillow under Jesus' head where he lay sleeping in the stern as the storm came up, but his head we never see. We know nothing of how he sounded when he talked, how he looked when he was asleep or awake, the slope of his shoulders when he was tired. Yet we know much without seeing, of course. We know him as we know all of them, as we know God, through their *dabharim*—through the words they speak which are also their deeds.

The Bible is full of their marvelous words. Isaac, hoodwinked into thinking that it is Esau who is kneeling before him instead of Jacob dressed up in Esau's clothes, sniffs the air as he blesses him and says, "See, the smell of my son is as the smell of the field that the Lord has blessed" (Genesis

27:27), and suddenly the blind old man is there before us in chiaroscuro as rich and moving as even Rembrandt could have managed it. "Oh my son Absalom, my son, my son. Would I had died instead of you, O Absalom, my son, my son"—we see, without seeing, all that is most kingly about David as well as all that is most human about him in those words he speaks when he learns that the son who betrayed him has fallen in battle; and we see Elijah's face in an ecstasy of derision as with scalding words he taunts the rival prophets whose frenzied efforts have all failed to persuade Baal to touch off the sacrificial pyre. "Cry aloud, for he is a god," Elijah says, his voice shrill with mockery. "Either he is musing, or he has gone aside, or he is on a journey, or perhaps he is asleep and must be awakened" (1 Kings 18:27). A camera could capture the scene no better.

There are also dialogues which not only evoke the character of the speakers but bring them alive before our eyes. Guiltily and in disguise King Saul goes at night to ask the witch of Endor to summon from the dead, old Samuel, who in life had been his friend, his conscience, his most implacable enemy.

> "Divine for me by a spirit, and bring up for me whomever I shall name to you."
> The woman said to him, "Surely you know what Saul has done, how he has cut off the mediums and the wizards from the land. Why then are you laying a snare for my life to bring about my death?"
> But Saul swore to her by the Lord, "As the Lord lives, no punishment shall come upon you for this thing."
> Then the woman said, "Whom shall I bring up for you?"
> He said, "Bring up Samuel for me."

When the woman saw Samuel, she cried out with a loud
voice, and the woman said to Saul, "Why have you deceived
me? You are Saul."

The king said to her, "Have no fear. What do you see?"

And the woman said to Saul, "I see a god coming up out
of the earth."

He said to her, "What is his appearance?"

And she said, "An old man is coming up, and he is
wrapped in a robe."

And Saul knew that it was Samuel, and he bowed with
his face to the ground and did obeisance. (1 Samuel
28:8–14)

Or take the words that Pilate and Jesus speak to each other
when they come face to face for the first time.

"Are you the King of the Jews?"

"Do you say this of your own accord, or did others say
it to you about me?"

"Am I a Jew? Your own nation and the chief priests have
handed you over to me. What have you done?"

"My kingship is not of this world. If my kingship were
of this world, my servants would fight that I might not be
handed over to the Jews, but my kingship is not from this
world."

"So you are a king?"

"You say that I am a king. For this I was born, and for
this I have come into the world, to bear witness to the
truth. Everyone who is of the truth hears my voice."

"What is truth?" (John 18:33–38)

It was by speaking his creative word into the primordial
darkness that God on the first day brought forth light, and
it is by speaking and listening to each other that out of the

darkness of our separate mysteries is brought to light the truth of who we are.

They speak, this huge gathering of people who crowd the pages of the Bible. They listen. They emerge, if we in turn listen to them, not as allegorical embodiments of Goodness and Badness but as flesh-and-blood men and women who no less ambiguously than the rest of us are good one day, bad the next, and occasionally both at once. Of all people in the world, Noah is the one who found favor with God, but Noah is also the one who quaffs so deeply of the fruit of his own vines that he passes out cold. No less a one than Father Abraham himself—the exemplar of faith, God's friend—willingly abandons the wife of his bosom to Pharaoh's harem rather than to risk his neck trying to save her. Jacob is a schemer and a crook, but he is also the one whom God visits with holy dreams and chooses over his blameless twin, Esau, to be Israel, the father of the twelve tribes and bearer of the promise. In religious art, the disciples of Jesus appear wearing halos, but in the Gospel story they are largely indistinguishable from everybody else— vying with each other for first place, continually missing the point, and, when the going gets rough, interested in nothing so much as saving their own skins down to the last man. Even Jesus himself comes through as far more complex and human than generations of piety have portrayed him. His fellow townspeople at Nazareth are so offended by him that they all but throw him headlong off a cliff. He speaks sharply if not downright heartlessly to his mother. When the full horror of what lies ahead comes through to him at Gethsemane, he sweats blood and pleads with God to let him off. As Mark tells it, the last words he ever spoke were not a ringing affirmation of faith but a cry of dereliction and despair.

Whatever else they may be, they are real human beings, in other words, and it is not the world of the Sunday school tract that they move through but a Dostoevskian world of darkness and light commingled, where suffering is sometimes redemptive and sometimes turns the heart to stone. It is a world where although God is sometimes to be known through his life-giving presence, there are other times when he is known only by his appalling absence. The Bible is a compilation of stories of what happened to these human beings in such a world, and the stories are not only as different from one another as the people they are about but are told in almost as many different ways. Side by side in the opening pages of Genesis, for instance, there are two stories of the creation, one of them as stately and rhythmic as plainsong, the other as homely and human as the way you might tell it to your grandchildren. The groups of stories about Jacob and his son Joseph, told in as unpretentious a style as the second creation story, are nonetheless complex, full of psychological motivation and rich with detail; and in the case of Jacob in particular, no character in fiction is more multifaceted, fascinating, or believable.

In a different style altogether is, say, the story of Nebuchadnezzar's golden idol as it appears in the Book of Daniel.

> King Nebuchadnezzar made an image of gold, whose
> height was sixty cubits and its breadth six cubits. He set it
> up on the plain of Dura, in the province of Babylon. Then
> King Nebuchadnezzar sent to assemble the satraps, the pre-
> fects, and the governors, the counselors, the treasurers, the

justices, the magistrates, and all the officials of the provinces to come to the dedication of the image which King Nebuchadnezzar had set up. Then the satraps, the prefects, and the governors, the counselors, the treasurers, the justices, the magistrates, and all the officials of the provinces, were assembled for the dedication of the image that King Nebuchadnezzar had set up; and they stood before the image that Nebuchadnezzar had set up. And the herald proclaimed aloud, "You are commanded, O peoples, nations, and languages, that when you hear the sound of the horn, pipe, lyre, trigon, harp, bagpipe, and every kind of music, you are to fall down and worship the golden image that King Nebuchadnezzar has set up; and whoever does not fall down and worship shall immediately be cast into a burning fiery furnace." Therefore, as soon as all the peoples heard the sound of the horn, pipe, lyre, trigon, harp, bag-pipe, and every kind of music, all the people fell down and worshiped the golden image which King Nebuchadnezzar had set up. (Daniel 3:2–7)

Here all is sophisticated artistry—the wondrously satiric effect of those sonorous, deadpan repetitions of musical instruments and officials which continue to occur through-out the story, for example, and the way each time the words "the image which King Nebuchadnezzar set up" appear, they manage to convey again not only that all the setting up in the world will fail to prevent the golden image from someday tumbling down but that even on a Babylonian scale all human glory in general is a vain and transitory thing. Not even the Book of Ecclesiastes conveys it better. The author of the Book of Job takes an ancient folktale and with a different kind of artistry entirely uses it as the frame for his fathomless poem which comes closer to classic drama than any other work that Israel produced. The mission of Israel is to preach God's mercy to all nations, and to dramatize that point the author of the Book of Jonah tells a story which seems to me to come closer than anything else in the Bible to high comedy—the recalcitrant prophet preaching salvation to the heathen while grumbling all the way, and God at the end pretending to mistake Jonah's anger at the sun for scorching him as pity for the shriveled vine that no longer gives him shade.

In the realm of historical as distinct from fictional narrative, the apparently eyewitness account in 2 Samuel 9–20 and 1 Kings 1–2 of the intrigues of David's court is as psychologically convincing, thorough, and full of life as any history the ancient world produced. One thinks also of the unforgettable portrait it provides of the ruthless, emotional, vulnerable character of David himself, who could order Uriah's murder without batting an eye yet give sanctuary to the crippled son of his dead friend Jonathan, and of the particularly vivid account of the last years of his reign when Bathsheba was nagging him about the succession and not even having the beautiful young Abishag for a bedmate was able to drive the chill of approaching death out of his old bones.

There could hardly be a greater miscellany of stories, characters, styles than are contained in this massive volume. There could hardly be a greater divergence among the ways God is portrayed—vindictive and bellicose, loving and merciful—or the ways human beings are portrayed either and the ways God is shown as wanting them to be related to him and to each other. Yet for all of that, the whole great drama somehow holds together.

Genesis is part of what does it—the prologue in which the stage is set and all the major themes first introduced. And the major themes themselves are part—creation, covenant, law, sin, grace, weaving in and out through all the histories and stories, all the poems, psalms, prophecies. And the leading characters are part: God in his holiness pervading every page, and such heroes of the faith as the Epistle to the Hebrews lists—Abraham and Sarah, Moses and Rahab, David and Samuel and the prophets—who both appear in their places and then keep on reappearing in the long memory of their people. And for Christians, of course, Jesus holds it together because it is both his Bible and the Bible about him.

Finally I think it is possible to say that in spite of all its extraordinary variety, the Bible is held together by having a single plot. It is one that can be simply stated: God creates the world, the world gets lost; God seeks to restore the world to the glory for which he created it. That means that the Bible is a book about you and me, whom he also made and lost and continually seeks, so you might say that what holds it together more than anything else is us. You might add to that, of course, that of all the books that humanity has produced, it is the one which more than any other—and in more senses than one—also holds us together.

3

Paul Sends His Love

The Greek rhetorician Alciphron wrote in his memoirs, "Never yet have I been to Corinth, for I know pretty well the beastly kind of life the rich enjoy there and the wretchedness of the poor," and from the time of Aristophanes on the city could even claim the distinction of having its name made into a verb. To "corinthianize" meant to go to the dogs. Situated on the narrow isthmus that connects Greece proper with the Peloponnesus, it was a major center for trade and shipping. Its population was largely immigrant, and sailors from everywhere under the sun prowled its streets bringing their gods with them—Isis and Serapis from Egypt, Astarte from Syria, Artemis from Ephesus to name just a few. The most striking geographical feature of the place was a steeply rising peak known as Acrocorinth, and on its summit—to symbolize her ascendancy both over all rivals and in the hearts of the citizenry—there stood a temple to the goddess Aphrodite which according to the Greek historian Strabo employed the services of some one thousand sacred prostitutes. "Not every man should go to Corinth" was an ancient byword whose reasonableness seems beyond challenge.

Saint Paul should have taken it to heart. Around A.D. 50 he arrived there for the first time, and the book of Acts gives a brief but vivid account of the consequences. He went to live with a Jewish couple named Priscilla and Aquila—leather workers like him—who had left Rome when the Emperor Claudius ordered all Jews out. They introduced him to the local synagogue, and as a distinguished guest he was invited to address the congregation. His zealous promotion of the claim that a Nazarene named Jesus, only some twenty years earlier crucified in Jerusalem, was the Messiah and Lord of life of ancient Jewish expectation so horrified some of the synagogue leaders that as a blasphemer and heretic they told him to leave and never show his face again. This he did but not before taking with him a number of Jews he had converted to the new faith including a man named Crispus, the synagogue's ruler. In the house of one Titus Justus, who to add insult to injury was the synagogue's next door neighbor, he set up a Christian church where for a year and a half he preached the Gospel until he decided to continue his missionary activities elsewhere. This journey eventually landed him across the Aegean in the city of Ephesus, and it was there a few years later that he received from the converts he had left behind in Corinth a letter which First Corinthians is in part an answer to.

Paul's responses to the specific questions that they posed and to the local problems they asked him to advise them on by no means constitute the most important or interesting part of the epistle, but they give a rich sense of the kind of document it was written to be. Paul was not primarily concerned with setting forth religious doctrine as he did in Romans and Galatians. He made no attempt to present an

orderly résumé of the Christian faith. He was simply trying
to set his Corinthian friends straight on the concrete matters that immediately concerned them and only in the process of doing that got sidetracked into some of the most
eloquent, moving, and self-revelatory passages that he ever
wrote.

You can't help wishing you knew more about those concrete matters. There is just enough here to tantalize. Was the
Sosthenes he mentions in his opening salutation the same
Sosthenes that the Corinthian Jews beat up after their
unsuccessful attempt to get Paul into trouble with the
Roman proconsul Gallio, who threw the whole pack of them
out of court saying in so many words that the internecine
squabbles of the Jews bored him to death? And how about
Chloe, whose "people"—slaves? household members?—
brought Paul news in Ephesus of certain goings-on which
the Corinthians themselves had apparently chosen not to
mention in their letter? She seems to have been one of the
few well-heeled members of a congregation which otherwise,
Paul tells us, consisted mainly of the lower orders, the more
or less down and out. It would be especially interesting to
know more about Apollos, an Alexandrian Jew who preached
in Corinth after Paul's departure. Is it possible that Paul's
disparagement of philosophical eloquence and, in second
Corinthians, his acerbic reference to "super apostles" are
allusions to him? Is it conceivable that Luther was right in
identifying him, not Paul, as the one who wrote the eloquent
Epistle to the Hebrews? Or, as others have believed, was it
Priscilla, Paul's hostess, who wrote it? Her name is mentioned ahead of her husband's in the passage in Acts that
describes them as the ones who took Apollos aside and

"expounded to him the way of God more accurately," suggesting perhaps that theologically speaking anyway she was the one who called the shots in the family. In any case they were both of them with Paul in Ephesus when he wrote his letter, and he sends their greetings back home along with his own.

But if Paul gives us only a fragmentary picture of the dramatis personae, he leaves us in no doubt as to the general situation they were involved in. It is clear that one way or another all hell had broken loose. Foreshadowing the fate of Christendom from then on, the small church had already split up into a number of factions. One of them followed Paul himself, another his successor Apollos, another the apostle Peter, and a fourth Christ, whoever these last could have been, possibly a group of Christian Gnostics who denied the humanity of Jesus. There had also sprung up a group of charismatics or *pneumatikoi*, who claimed to have such spiritual gifts as speaking with tongues and "prophecy" and who seem to have been given not only to playing at spiritual one-upmanship with each other but to looking down their noses at pretty much everybody else. One member of the congregation and his stepmother were living together as man and wife despite the fact that Roman as well as Jewish law condemned such a relationship. Others were gorging themselves and getting drunk at the Lord's Supper, which at this early point was not the ritual wafer and sip of wine that it later became but still a full meal that the whole church ate together presumably in the house of one of its members. And so on. Things couldn't have been much worse. Paul wrote that he could not "address [them] as spiritual men, but as men of the flesh, as babes in Christ, for while there is jealousy and strife among you, are you not of the flesh and behaving like ordinary men?"

Jealousy and strife were almost the least of it. The Church in Corinth and everywhere else for that matter was indeed ordinary men and women who spiritually speaking hadn't cut their first teeth yet. It was slaves, dock hands, shopkeepers, potters, housewives, bronze workers, leather workers, and what have you. They were no better than anybody else and at least in one sense worse because, "sanctified in Christ Jesus" as Paul believed them to be, so much more was expected of them and should have been forthcoming. They were in fact Christ's body as he wrote them here in one of his most enduring metaphors—Christ's eyes, ears, hands—but the way they were carrying on, that could only leave Christ bloodshot, ass-eared, all thumbs, to carry on God's work in a fallen world. What came forth from them was just the kind of wretched tangle they were in at the moment and, harder still for him to deal with, the wretchedness it gave rise to within himself. It is this which in many ways is what First Corinthians is essentially about—his sense of futility and despair at war with his exultant hope, the terrible tension between the *in spite of* and the *because of* of his restless and often anguished faith.

He fielded their questions as best he could—questions about sex and marriage, about the role of women in church, about whether or not it was proper to eat meat which in a gentile city like Corinth had probably all been dedicated to some godling or other down to the last lamb chop. His answers tend to be pedagogic, avuncular, appealing more to tradition than to theology. It was better to marry than to burn, he told them in a phrase that has echoed down the centuries. Women should be veiled in church and not speak. It couldn't matter less that the meat they ate had already been offered up to Serapis or Astarte—that was just the sort of religious pedantry that Christ had set them free from— but if by eating it they shook the faith of some Christian friend to whom it did matter, then of course they should abstain for the friend's sake. But there is no mistaking that for Paul the real question lay deeper down than any of these. "The word of the cross is folly to those who are perishing," he wrote. Was it possible that it was folly, period? It seems clear enough that in his heart of hearts that was the question that haunted him above all others.

The message that a convicted felon was the bearer of God's forgiving and transforming love was hard enough for anybody to swallow and for some especially so. For Helle- nized sophisticates—the Greeks, as Paul puts it—it could only seem absurd. What uglier, more supremely inappropri- ate symbol of, say, Plato's Beautiful and Good could there be than a crucified Jew? And for the devout Jew, what more scandalous image of the Davidic King-Messiah, before whose majesty all the nations were at last to come to heel? Paul understood both reactions well. "The folly of what we preach," he called it, and he knew it was folly not just to the intellectually and religiously inclined but to the garden vari- ety Corinthians who had no particular pretensions in either direction but simply wanted some reasonably plausible god who would stand by them when the going got rough. Paul's God didn't look much like what they were after, and Paul was the first to admit it. Who stood by Jesus when the going got rough, after all? He even goes so far as to speak of "the fool-ishness of God." What other way could you describe a deity who chose as his followers not the movers and shakers who could build him a temple to make Aphrodite's look like two cents but the weak, the despised, the ones who were foolish even as their God was and poor as churchmice?

To pray for your enemies, to worry about the poor when you have worries enough of your own, to start becoming yourself fully by giving of yourself prodigally to whoever needs you, to love your neighbors when an intelligent fourth-grader could tell you that the way to get ahead in the world is to beat your neighbors to the draw every chance you get—that was what this God asked, Paul wrote. That was who this God was. That was who Jesus was. Paul is passionate in his assertion of course, that in the long run it is such worldly wisdom as the intelligent fourth-grader's that is foolish and the sublime foolishness of God that is ultimately wise, and nobody heard him better than William Shakespeare did when he wove the rich fabric of *King Lear* around precisely this para-dox. It is the Fool, Edgar, Kent, Cordelia, Gloucester—the foolish, weak, despised ones—who in their fatal loyalty to the ruined king triumph, humanly speaking, over the powerful cunning of Regan, Goneril, Edmund, and the rest of them. "Upon such sacrifices, my Cordelia, the gods themselves throw incense." Lear says to Cordelia—that is their tri-umph—just as, before him, Paul quoted Isaiah's, "What no eye has seen, nor ear heard, nor the heart of man conceived, [that is] what God has prepared for those who love him."

But Paul was as aware as Shakespeare was that when the final curtain rings down, the ones who loved this God of love end up just as dead as the ones who never gave him the time of day, and he was aware that any Corinthians shopping around for a new religion were aware of it too. So it was a matter of not only what could look more foolish than the Gospel he preached but perhaps even of what could actually *be* more foolish. Terrible as that possibility was, he did not flinch from putting it down in black and white. "If for this life only we have hoped in Christ," he wrote, "we are of all men most to be pitied."

He must have considered the possibility that, as Edmund believed, the only God worth a hoot is the god of raw Nature, that it is the fittest not the fairest who survive longest, and that in the long run the only law that matters is the law of the jungle. "If Christ has not been raised," he flatly said, "then our preaching is in vain and your faith is in vain. . . . If the dead are not raised, 'Let us eat and drink, for tomorrow we die.' " It is impossible to read these words without having the sense that he is speaking here not just theologically, apodictically, but personally, out of his own darkest misgivings. "We are fools for Christ's sake," he wrote, meaning fools as holy as Christ himself was holy. But if Christ ended up as dead as everybody else, then he knew they were also damned fools and Christ himself had been fooled most tragically. "To the present hour we hunger and thirst, we are ill-clad and buffeted and homeless. . . . We have become, and are now, as the refuse of the world, the off-scouring of all things." That is how he described his life as apostle to the gentiles, but it was the inner buffeting and homelessness that were the worst of it.

Paul was no beauty if the description of him in the apocryphal *Acts of Paul and Thecla* is to be believed. "Bald-headed, bowlegged, strongly built, a man small in size, with meeting eyebrows, with a rather large nose. His letters are strong, but his bodily presence is weak." You see those meeting eyebrows knotted, see the way he holds his bald head in his hands, his rather large nose lost in shadow, as he writes out of his grimness. But something extraordinary keeps him going on those bow legs of his anyway, in spite of everything. He has himself seen Christ after the crucifixion. That is what keeps him going through thick and thin. That is what keeps him firing off his letters like rockets.

In this letter he does not describe what it was like to see Christ, he simply states it as a fact, but it is described elsewhere, and doubtless he told them about it in Corinth when he was there ... the light that blinded him for days afterward, the voice calling him by name. He never forgot the sheer and giddy grace of it, of Christ appearing to him of all people, professional persecutor of Christians as he was at the time; of Christ not only forgiving him but enlisting him, signing him up as Apostle to the Gentiles. Everything Paul ever did or wrote from that moment on flamed up out of that extraordinary encounter on the Damascus road. And there was something else if anything even more extraordinary. If death was not the end of Christ, then it was not to be the end of any of them. "For as in Adam all die, so also in Christ shall all be made alive." They were all of them *in Christ*—one of his favorite phrases—as Christ was also in all of them, and thus life, not death, was to be the last thing for them too. Nor was it to be some disembodied life either as the Greek dualists argued with their dim view of bodies generally, but life as themselves, wearing some marvelous new version of corporeality, not of flesh and blood any longer but of "spirit ... imperishable ... raised in Glory."

"Lo! I tell you a mystery." His tone becomes lyric, exultant. "We shall all be changed, in a moment, in the twinkling of an eye, at the last trumpet. . . . Thanks be to God, who gives us the victory. . . . Therefore, my beloved brethren, be steadfast, immovable, always abounding in the work of the Lord, knowing that in the Lord your labor is not in vain." The great nostrils swell.

That is the farthest and deepest his eyes have seen, farther even than the depths of the dark, the brightest thing he has to tell. Then in the next breath he is down to brass tacks again, explaining to them how the money for the Jerusalem church is to be collected, how it is to be sent there, where he plans to travel next and when. Who knows when the last trumpet will sound? In the meanwhile, for all of them, there is much work to be done. Yet in the meanwhile too—he has already written them of this—there is much to rejoice in this side of the great Joy.

There is among other things the Lord's Supper, which some of the Corinthians have been turning into a three-ring circus. He berates them at first. The sentences are short and sharp. They have behaved outrageously. He is outraged. "What shall I say to you?" Then abruptly the language changes and his tone with it. The words start to come with a kind of twilight hush to them. They have an almost dazed quality, as if he is so caught up in the scene he is describing that he is more there than here. He hadn't actually been there, of course, but he knew some who had been—like Peter, for instance, his old colleague and sometime adversary. Peter must have spoken of what he remembered about the last time they had all of them eaten together with Jesus, and it is such memories as his that Paul is presumably drawing on here though that is not what he says. He "received [it] of the Lord," is what he says. Who knows what he means—that it was the significance of that last meal, the full truth of those last words, that he received perhaps. In any case, he remembers details, remembers that the night of his betrayal was when it happened, remembers how the bread was taken, broken, thanked for, remembers the wine. It is the first time you realize fully how few years had gone by since it all happened. There were men and women around still who had eaten and drunk with Jesus if not that final meal, who knew the sound of his voice, could have picked him out in a crowd. Paul remembers what he said. That the bread was his body. The wine was his blood. It was he himself they were eating and drinking, taking his life into their lives, into them. This meal was their proclamation of what his death had done and meant, and for anybody to make a drunken shambles of it was to risk sickness and death. It was their consolation and the Lord's great gift to them till he came back again in his glory. And there were other gifts.

Not even in the Gospels is there a more familiar passage than the thirteenth chapter of First Corinthians. "Though I speak with the tongues of men and of angels . . . when I was a child, I spake as a child . . . through a glass darkly. . . ." Words as familiar as these are like coins worn smooth with long handling. After a while it is hard to tell where they came from or what they are worth. Paul has been speaking about spiritual gifts—prophecy, tongues, healing, miracles, and so on—and making the point that they should not be the cause of still further divisiveness, people gifted one way disparaging people gifted another. He sees all Christians as parts of Christ's body and each part in its own way as necessary as every other. "The eye cannot say to the hand, 'I have no need of you.'" Each gift is to be cherished. "But," he says then, "earnestly desire the higher gifts" and at that point sets off into what turned out to be perhaps the most memorable words he ever wrote.

The highest gift of all is *agape*, he says. Without it even faith, almsgiving, martyrdom, are mere busyness and even great wisdom doesn't amount to a hill of beans. The translators of the King James version render the Greek word as "charity," which in seventeenth-century usage was a happy choice—charity as the beneficence of the rich to the poor, the lucky to the unlucky, the powerful to the weak, the lovely to the unlovely. But since to our age the word all too often suggests a cheerless and demeaning handout, modern translators have usually rendered it as "love." But *agape* love is not to be confused with *eros* love. That is what Paul is at such pains to make clear here.

Eros love is love that reaches upwards. It is love for what we need to fill our emptiness, love for what is lovely and lovable. It is Dante's love for Beatrice as well as Cleopatra's for Antony, the child's love for the parent, humankind's love for God. William Blake engraved the picture of a tiny human figure with a ladder pitched toward the moon and underneath, in block capitals, the words I WANT! I WANT! Those are the words that *eros* always speaks. Not so with *agape*. *Agape* does not want. It gives. It is not empty. It is full to overflowing. Paul strains to get the distinction right. *Agape* is patient; *eros* champs at the bit. *Agape* puts up with anything; *eros* insists on having things its own way. *Agape* is kind—never jealous, boastful, rude. It does not love *because* but simply loves—the way the rain falls or the sun shines. It

"bears all things," up to and including even its own crucifixion. And it has extraordinary power.

The power of *agape*—otherwise quite powerless—is perhaps nowhere better seen than in the tale of *Beauty and the
Beast*, where Beauty does not love the Beast because he is
beautiful but makes him beautiful by loving him. Ultimately,
in other words, *agape* is God's love for humankind, and only
as God's gift are humans enabled at rare moments to love
that way themselves—transformingly, unconditionally, no
matter what. Thus when Paul says, "Love never ends," he is
not being sentimental or merely rhetorical. There is no
doubt that *eros* ends. Even in its noblest forms it ends when
the desired becomes undesirable or when desire ends. *Agape*,
on the other hand, is as without end as God is without end
because it is of the essence of God. That is what Paul experienced on the Damascus road where he found that the One
who had every cause to deplore him loved him. For as long
as the moment lasted anyway, the beetle-browed, bowlegged
Christian-baiter put away his own childish things and in an
unutterable instant saw Truth itself not through a glass
darkly for once but face to face; understood, as he put it,
even as he was understood.

He himself was the first to admit that he remained in
many ways as much of a mess as the rest of us—full of
anguished doubts and depressions, hostilities, exaltations,
hang-ups, whatever he meant by "the thorn in the flesh,"
which he interpreted in his second letter to Corinth as
God's way of keeping him "from being too elated." The bitter and the better of him, it is all there in the words with
which he closes his letter, the words which he tells us he is
writing with his own hand.

"If any one has no love for the Lord, let him be accursed. Our Lord, come. The grace of the Lord be with you." A malediction, a prayer, a benediction, in that order. They are all mixed up together as God knows they were all mixed up in Paul himself. But then, "My love be with you all in Christ Jesus. Amen," so that the very last thing of all that he does is send them his love—*agape* is again the word he uses—the most precious thing he ever received, the most precious thing he ever had to give.

4

The Emerald City:
A Commencement Address

I don't know where you members of the graduating class were in the year 1932, but I know where I was. I'm not sure about 1931 or 1933, but 1932 I remember very clearly.

I was six years old at the time, and I was sick in bed off and on for more or less the whole year with a series of things wrong with me like pneumonia and pleurisy and tonsillitis and the like. Television hadn't been invented yet, and I don't think there was anything much on the radio to interest six-year-olds either, so the only thing I had for whiling away the long, dreary days was books, and the books I loved better than all others were the Oz books. They were still coming out at the rate of about one a year back in those ancient times, and either I read them to myself or got other people to read them to me, and the world they were about was so much more real and interesting to me than the world of nurses and doctors and croup kettles and mustard plasters that the place I really lived that year was Oz. I came to know a great many of its inhabitants very well while I was there, and the one I want to present for your particular consideration this Commencement Day is the Wizard of Oz himself. I'm sure you've all seen the movie even if you haven't read the book, so I'll get directly to the point and just tell you that the most important thing about the Wizard is that he was above all else a man of surprises. I'm thinking of two surprises in particular.

The first surprise comes, of course, when Dorothy and her three friends discover that he's not really a wizard at all. You remember the scene. Oz the Great and Terrible, as he liked to call himself, turns out not to be in any way either great or terrible. He is just a rather short old man with a bald head and wrinkles who stands behind the screen in the throne room working the machine that creates various illusions like an enormous ball of fire and a huge green head which everybody thinks is the Wizard himself until Dorothy's dog, Toto, accidentally knocks the screen over and the cat is out of the bag at last. The Scarecrow tells the Wizard he ought to be ashamed of himself for being such a humbug, and the old man makes no attempt to deny it. He says that he was born in Omaha, Nebraska, and that he used to be a pretty good ventriloquist. He also says that he used to go up in a hot air balloon to draw crowds for a circus, and that was how he happened to drift into Oz in the first place. The Wizard of Oz is not the kind of wizard that everybody thought he was. That is surprise number one.

Surprise number two is even more surprising, and it is this. In the ordinary abracadabra, presto-changeo sense of the word, the Wizard of Oz is not a wizard at all. But in another sense, he is not only a very great wizard indeed but the worker of magic which no one should be allowed to graduate from anywhere without knowing about. What makes him such a wizard is that he has X-ray eyes, and what he sees when he looks at the three oddballs standing before him with their various problems is something that nobody else can see. But before I get back to that, take a look at those three oddballs themselves for a minute.

The Scarecrow, for instance. Everybody knows what the Scarecrow's problem is. His problem is that he doesn't have any brains, or at least he thinks he doesn't. That's the problem of scarecrows generally, of course, including any that happen to be graduating today. Some people go through school like a breeze. They get good grades without half trying. For them even something like calculus is a piece of cake. When a teacher asks a question, their hands shoot up before the teacher has finished asking it, and nine times out of ten they answer it right. They get their papers in on time. They apply for early admission to places like Brown and Yale and Harvard, and they get accepted. They win prizes.

If you're a scarecrow, on the other hand, you don't see how they do it. For you, nothing is a breeze. There's no such thing as a piece of cake. When teachers ask questions, you're as good at not catching their eyes as a waiter in a crowded restaurant. Even if you get a week's extension on a paper, you have a hunch it's hardly worth finishing because all the time you're writing it, you keep thinking how much better a job your smart friends would do. Whenever you get a crummy grade, it only makes you the surer that a scarecrow is what you are and a scarecrow is what you'll always be. If and when you ever get accepted by a college somewhere, you have the feeling you'll probably squeak by again with another diploma after another four years of grinding away at it, but then you see your real problems just beginning. What kind of a job can a scarecrow hope to land? What kind of a salary can a scarecrow expect to earn? Where is a scarecrow going to end up in the great rat race? Life is a scary business for anybody let alone for people who suspect they have nothing but straw where their brains belong. It's very scary and it's also very depressing, and if you should happen to wonder why I speak with such feeling, it's because of course I've always been a scarecrow myself. I figure most people I meet have more brains than I do. If there are questions being asked, I always hope somebody else will answer them. I rarely if ever win prizes.

I speak as a scarecrow to scarecrows, and I also speak to any Cowardly Lions and Tin Woodsmen of either gender who happen to be among you. I suppose the mark of a Cowardly Lion is that you think about the great world out there and worry not so much that you don't have brains enough to handle it as that you don't have guts enough to survive in it. I remember when I was your age I'd look at people of my parents' generation and wonder how on earth they managed to do it. They kept the wolf from the door. They raised children. They acquired houses and automobiles and electric refrigerators and kept them more or less in repair. They held down jobs and got their taxes paid. Generally speaking they seemed to be in charge of their lives and independent and resourceful and able to cope with reality in ways that I couldn't believe I'd ever be capable of myself even if I had a hundred years to work at it.

And the Tin Woodsman? If you're a Tin Woodsman, you're convinced that you're a kind of a freak. The Tin Woodsman believed he didn't have a heart like other people, and you believe you're lacking something equally basic. For instance, you're not sure you *feel* the way human beings are supposed to feel. Some of the things that make other people laugh make you want to cry, and sometimes the other way round too. You don't make friends as easily as you wish you did, and there are times when you feel like a creature from another planet. There are times when like E.T. you want to phone home, but you're not sure where you belong or exactly what home is. If you're a Tin Woodsman, you can be lonely even when you're surrounded by people you've known all your life. You wonder if anybody is ever going to love you the way you read about it in books. You wonder if you're ever going to find anybody you can love that way yourself. To one degree or another we're all of us Tin Woodsmen, of course, just as we're all of us Scarecrows and Cowardly Lions, too. We all have our moments of feeling out of place and left out.

And now back to the small bald man with wrinkles again, the one behind the screen. The first surprise happens when he turns out to be no wizard at all and the second when he turns out to be a very great wizard indeed because he has X-ray eyes. And the magic he can work with those X-ray eyes of his is to look at those three strange characters standing in front of him and, beneath what they're afraid they are, to see deep down inside to what they really are. And what he sees they really are, of course, is absolutely wonderful. The Scarecrow may not have a brain just like everybody else's—who wants a brain just like everybody else's?—but he has a wonderful brain all his own as everything he's done up this point richly demonstrates. Far from being a coward, the Lion is brave enough to act bravely even when he's scared half out of his wits, which is what true bravery is all about. And as for the Tin Woodsman, despite all his fears he has a heart so human and tender that they have to keep using the oil can on him to keep him from being rusted by his own tears.

But the greatest thing about the Wizard of Oz's wizardry is that he doesn't just see how wonderful the three of them are inside themselves but actually brings the wonderfulness out. He helps them to become as wonderful as they actually are. Do you remember that part of the movie? The Wizard gives the Lion a medal to wear. He gives the Tin Woodsman a sort of heart-shaped locket to hang around his neck. He gives the Scarecrow a diploma, appropriately enough. The things he gives aren't especially marvelous in themselves, but the magic of them is that they make it possible for those three odd characters to discover that they themselves are marvelous. By handing out his trinkets he goes beyond just seeing who they are at their best and in a way blesses who they are at their best. He brings forth in all of them the magic they already have and already are. And that is what education literally means. To educate (*ex* + *ducere*) means to lead or bring forth, and the whole point of education is to bring forth all the wisdom and courage and humanity that are part of who you are even though there are lots of times when you simply can't believe that they are. What you learn from books ultimately, or what you learn from them if you're taught right, is not just the riches of the past—of history, science, literature, and all that—but your own riches. The world is as scary as all get-out for all of us and maybe especially scary for you because to graduate from school is to come one giant step closer to getting out into the thick of things. Everybody is putting pressure on you to make your mark in this scary world, and most of all you put pressure on yourselves—to be smart, to be strong, to be successful and popular. But the absolutely fundamental purpose of education, as I see it anyway, is to show you that what's most important of all is to be the one thing that nobody else in the whole wide world can be except you, and that is your own unique and precious self. Whatever you *do* with your life—whatever you end up achieving or not achieving—the great gift you have in you to give to the world is the gift of who you alone are: your way of seeing things, and saying things, and feeling about things, that is like nobody else's. If so much as a single one of you were missing, there would be an empty place at the great feast of life that nobody else in all creation could fill.

Finally let me remind you of another wizard even greater than the Wizard of Oz who was also a man of many surprises and who in many ways says the same thing. He also has X-ray eyes, and just as he once looked out at his little band of followers a long time ago and a long way away, so he looks out at young scarecrows and lions and tin men and tin women like you, and at old scarecrows and lions and tin men like me, and says: Be not afraid. You are the light of the world. You are the salt of the earth.

"The Kingdom of God is within you" is another way Jesus said it, that greatest of all wizards, and nowhere in Heaven or on earth is there a magic greater than his to bring that truth forth in each of us, to make that inner kingdom come. So here at the end it is to his love, and his care, and his holy wizardry that I commend you as the best graduation present I have to give. May you be brave and wise and human all the way through, and may all of you find your way to the Emerald City at last.

5

Flannery O'Connor

I came to Flannery O'Connor late, not until fifteen years or more after her death. I was often told I should read her because like me she was, Heaven help us, a *religious* writer. People who read her books also sometimes read mine. I even came across occasional articles which touched on us both. We worked the same territory. And that was of course just the trouble. It's hard enough to work a territory under the best of circumstances let alone with one eye cocked on somebody else working in the next cotton patch. Was she doing it better than I was? In what ways was she doing it differently? Did she approach things, see things, feel things at all as I did, especially religious things? Whatever the answers were, I didn't want to know them. I didn't want to be distracted or deflected. I didn't want to be threatened. I just wanted to keeping on working my own little plot. And then one day, I forget just how or why, I read her story "A Good Man Is Hard to Find."

I can still remember the impact of it: the killing comedy of the family taking off on its jaunt with the children squabbling in the back seat, the beleaguered father, the loquacious grandmother with her "big black valise that looked like the head of a hippopotamus," and then suddenly the appearance of the scholarly-looking Misfit in his silver-rimmed spectacles and long creased face, his tan and white shoes with no socks. Except perhaps for Shirley Jackson's "The Lottery," I know of no story by anybody that so devastatingly catches you off guard with its ending, although needless to say you are given every reason to be on guard right from the start if you have your wits about you. I knew immediately that she was a wonder, an original. There could be no doubt about that. She was no threat to me or anybody else because her corner of the territory was one that no other writer in Christendom either could possibly work or as far as I know has ever worked, and because it is impossible to imagine her choosing to work any other. From that story on I was hooked, not just by the stories themselves but by the whole tragicomic red-clay world they come out of and that so richly comes out of them—the fierce old men, the impossible old women and their doomed sons, the ancient children, the oddballs, the crazy, tormented saints, and always, always, the wild, ragged figure of Jesus moving from tree to tree, as she describes it, in the back not only of Hazel Motes's mind but of every tale this extraordinary and Christ-possessed woman ever wrote.

"That belief in Christ is to some a matter of life and death has been a stumbling block for readers who would prefer to think of it as a matter of no great consequence," Flannery O'Connor wrote in a note to the second edition of *Wise Blood*. The wonder of it is that even among readers like that her reputation stands high. Intellectuals who otherwise steer a very wide berth indeed around religion of any kind claim her as their own. She is admired by people as ignorant of Christian thought as Eudora Welty claimed to be in an interview where she said that it was only her enthusiasm for O'Connor that led her to look up what the concept of *grace* was all about. The reason for her popularity in such circles is not hard to find. Perhaps most of all it has to do with the way she writes. Her taut, strong, relentlessly aimed style with all its concreteness and vividness is about as far as you can get from the overripe banalities usually associated with literary piety. And so, of course, is her wit.

I suppose it is precisely because she has a mystic's sense of what holiness truly is that she is able to depict in such a wry and sometimes uproarious way the freakish distortions that it suffers at the hands of a mad world. Her laughter comes from a very deep and holy place inside herself, in other words, and that is probably why it is so deeply infectious, why the comic element of her work is not merely one of its embellishments but of its very substance, as inseparable from the tragic element as grace is from sin. In addition to everything else she is, she is surely one of the most profoundly *funny* writers this century has yet produced. Anybody who doubts that has only to read "The Enduring Chill," for instance, where the baby-faced doctor, the unlettered Jesuit, and the two feckless blacks bring to ailing young Asbury, who is alone in believing that he is on his deathbed, exactly what he wants least and, if his soul is to be saved, exactly what he needs most.

If God is to save souls, he must do so with people who for the most part fight tooth and nail against the process. Hazel Motes ends up a kind of saint in spite of himself. Francis Marion Tarwater does everything he can to avoid becoming the prophet he is destined to be. Human life is so grotesquely distorted and distorting that the grace of God is broken to pieces by it like light through a prism and reaches us looking like everything except what it is. The chance sight of the plaster figure of a Negro with one eye chipped white and holding a piece of plaster watermelon. The approach of an old woman who has just had a stroke lurching down the city pavement with her hair undone on one side. It is often through just such outlandish means of grace as these that we are to be saved if we are to be saved at all, and opposed to our saving is all the madness and perversity not only of the world which we inhabit but of the worlds which we carry around inside our skins, the worlds which inhabit us and which we are. That is Flannery O'Connor's vision of life under God, of life as God moves inexorably and elusively through the all but hidden depths of it. That is the territory she works.

In the index to her collected letters, *The Habit of Being*, there is one reference to me which says something to the effect that she never read anything by Frederick Buechner. Ah well. And what would she have thought of me if she had? Would she have found my books in any way to her liking, I wonder? Would she at least have recognized me as a fellow worker in the vineyard? Might we conceivably have become friends?

My wife and I detoured through her home town of Milledgeville, Georgia, once on our way north from Florida. We stopped at the public library in town, where I asked the librarian if she could tell us where Flannery O'Connor was buried. The cemetery was called Memory Hill, she said, and I could imagine just the kind of crooked smile that must have elicited from Flannery herself. When we got there, I told a black man working around the place which grave it was that we were looking for and asked if he could possibly tell us where it was. He gave the directions so readily that I asked him if other people came looking for it sometimes. About one or two a day he said. And there it was, her birth date carved into the stone just one year earlier than mine, her death date in 1964 when she was thirty-nine years old. Her father's grave was right beside it. Memory Hill.

From the cemetery, following the librarian's instructions, we drove past the Catholic church where she used to worship and on out to Andalusia, the farm where for years she and her mother had lived. We were leery about driving up the dirt road that leads to it from the highway, but there were no signs of life as far as we could see so we did it anyway. There were some cedar trees growing around it, and I assumed that one of them was the one where Robert Fitzgerald tells us her peacocks were given to roosting at night, turning the grass beneath it white with their droppings. The house itself looked deserted, a medium-sized white farmhouse with a screen porch in front and a flight of wooden steps leading up to it. I snapped a photograph of it. Nothing in the world looks much emptier than a house that is empty.

Standing there in the spring afternoon, I said some sort of a silent prayer for her. I wished of all things grace to her, of course, and peace. And I said the best I could by way of thanks—to the Lord and giver of Life for giving us her, to her for giving us a glimpse through all the freakishness and sadness of things down toward the glowing heart.

6

The Opening of Veins

As it has been explained to me, the Whiting awards are given each year to writers of "exceptional promise," and it is that phrase "exceptional promise" that I would like to make my point of departure because it immediately raises two serious questions in my mind. The first question is: Promise of what? The second question is: Exceptional in what way? Both of them make me quite nervous whenever I think about them. In fact there is something about writing in general that makes me quite nervous whenever I think about it, especially the kind that is called creative writing. It suggests that there are other kinds of writing, and the first one that occurs to me is of course "destructive writing."

I am sure everybody will agree that writing can be destructive. Peter Benchley's *Jaws*, for instance. I didn't actually read it, but the year the movie first came out I saw it in Chicago with my youngest daughter, Sharmy, who watched it through the buttonhole of my green linen jacket which, even as I was wearing it, she had tucked her head under for comfort and protection. For me and Sharmy and God only knows how many million others, *Jaws* destroyed for the rest of our lives a significant part of the pleasure of swimming in the ocean. Or from another part of the spectrum altogether, I think of the novels of Charles Williams, whom in some ways I admire very much. There are passages in those novels where the Christian faith, which I love and believe in as he did, somehow gets mixed up with the occult, the operatic, the Madame Blavatskyan, in ways which if they do not actually destroy at least seriously disturb my peace of mind the way bad dreams do when you can't quite remember them or quite forget them either.

So when I think of writers of exceptional promise, all these misgivings run through my head. Some promises are promises you wish had never been kept. Charlotte Brontë was exceptional and so was the Marquis de Sade. There is writing that creates and writing that destroys. Needless to say, I have absolutely no misgivings about the writers being honored here this evening. I am confident that they would not be awarded prizes as distinguished as these in a setting as venerable if they hadn't convinced everybody that they are exceptionally promising in only the most beneficent way. It is not about them that I am speaking but about writers and writing in general.

Sometime in the early 1950s, for two years running, I taught creative writing at the summer session of the Washington Square branch of N.Y.U. I taught the prose section, and the poetry section was taught one year by Horace Gregory and the next year by Oscar Williams—that small amiable man with the triangular face and pink eyelids of a clever mouse who used to turn up at cocktail parties with a brown paper bag full of copies of one or the other of his many anthologies, which he autographed and passed around with such abandon that it was said that rare book dealers would pay top dollar for a copy he never happened to have gotten his hands on. I was uneasy about teaching creative writing for a number of reasons, one of which was that I've never been sure that it is something that can really be taught—for better or worse, I don't think anybody ever taught it to me anyway—and another that I had absolutely no idea how to teach it right if it is. But my main uneasiness came from somewhere else. Suppose, I thought, that by some fluke I did teach it at least right enough so that maybe a couple of people, say, learned how to write with some real measure of effectiveness and power. The question then became for me, what were they going to write effectively and powerfully about? Suppose they chose to write effective and powerful racist tracts or sadistic pornography or novels about warped and unpleasant people doing warped and unpleasant things? Or, speaking less sensationally, suppose they used the skills I had somehow managed to teach them to write books simply for the sake of making a name for themselves, or making money, or making a stir. It seemed to me and still does that to teach people how to write well without knowing what they are going to write about is like teaching people how to shoot well without knowing what or whom they are going to shoot at.

What a writer chooses to write about concerns me a lot because I think writers can for better or worse do things to their audience that other kinds of artists for the most part can't. Painters hang their pictures on the wall, and when you look at those pictures, there is a certain space between you and them. The kind of light there is in that space, the presence maybe of other pictures hanging nearby or of other people wandering around, the angle of your vision, the kind of eyesight you have—all those other things are going on while you're standing there looking at the picture, and one way or another they all to some degree dissipate, aerate, insulate you a little against the effect the picture has upon you. With music it is more or less the same thing. You are in one place and the music is coming from another place, whether the other place is an orchestra or a radio or your fancy new compact disc system, and all the same kinds of distractions and conditions are involved there.

With that in mind, I think of painting and music as *subcutaneous* arts. They get under your skin. They may get deeper than that eventually, but it takes a while, and they get there to some extent tinged by if not diluted by the conditions under which you saw them or heard them. Writing on the other hand strikes me as *intravenous*. As you sit there only a few inches from the printed page, the words you read go directly into the bloodstream and go into it at full strength. More than the painting you see or the music you hear, the words you read become in the very act of reading them part of who you are, especially if they are the words of exceptionally promising writers. If there is poison in the words, you are poisoned; if there is nourishment, you are nourished; if there is beauty, you are made a little more beautiful. In Hebrew the word *dabhar* means both word and also deed. A word doesn't merely say something, it does something. It brings something into being. It makes something happen. What do writers want their books to make happen? It is not a question that I ever thought to raise in Washington Square forty years ago, but I wish I had.

What I am getting around to, of course, is talking about the kinds of books that seem to me worth all the trouble it takes to write them, let alone to read them, the kind of words suitable for injecting into the bloodstream of the world. I am thinking of all the things I wish I had known to say to the odd assortment of people who turned up at those long-ago N.Y.U. classes. There was one man who conceived the idea of rendering a character's thoughts vertically on the page so I had to keep turning his manuscripts sideways so I could read them. There was a short, plump German man who I believe was a baker, at least he looked like a baker, and a young man who had been James Farrell's secretary. I wish that I had told them to give some thought to what they wanted their books to make happen inside the people who read them, and I also wish that I had told them what Red Smith said about writing, although I suppose it is possible that he hadn't gotten around to saying it yet. As I am sure you all know, what Red Smith said was more or less this: "Writing is really quite simple; all you have to do is sit down at your typewriter and open a vein"—another hematological image. From the writer's vein into the reader's vein: for better or worse a transfusion.

I couldn't agree with Red Smith more. For my money anyway, the only books worth reading are books written in blood. I have always thought that the classic advice to write about what you know about is misleading because it seems to mean that if you come from the Middle West, say, you should write only about the Middle West, if you're black you should write only about blacks, and so forth. If you expand "what you know about" to include what you know about in your dreams, in your nightmares, in your stomach, then it's OK and lets Stephen Crane write *The Red Badge of Courage* and Gertrude Stein write *Three Lives* and Shakespeare write *The Tempest*. But the advice is ambiguous at best. Red Smith's advice, on the other hand, is clear as a bell.

Write about what you really care about is what he is saying. Write about what truly matters to you—not just things to catch the eye of the world but things to touch the quick of the world the way they have touched you to the quick, which is why you are writing about them. Write not just with wit and eloquence and style and relevance but with passion. Then the things that your books make happen will be things worth happening—things that make the people who read them a little more passionate themselves for their pains, by which I mean a little more alive, a little wiser, a little more beautiful, a little more open and understanding, in short a little more human. I believe that those are the best things that books can make happen to people, and we could all make a list of the particular books that have made them happen to us.

J. D. Salinger's *The Catcher in the Rye* was one of the first I read that did it to me, that started me on the long and God knows far from finished journey on the way to becoming a human being—started making *that* happen. What I chiefly learned from it was that even the slobs and phonies and morons that Holden Caulfield runs into on his travels are, like Seymour Glass's Fat Lady, "Christ Himself, buddy," as Zooey explains it to his sister Franny in the book that bears their names. Even the worst among us are precious. Even the most precious among us bear crosses. That was a word that went straight into my bloodstream and has been there ever since. Along similar lines I think also of Robertson Davies's Deptford trilogy, Ford Madox Ford's *The Good Soldier*, Rose Macaulay's *The Towers of Trebizond*, George Garrett's *Death of the Fox*, some of the early novels of John Updike like *The Poorhouse Fair* and *The Centaur*, John Irving's *A Prayer for Owen Meany*. I think of stories like Flannery O'Connor's "The Artificial Nigger" and Raymond Carver's "Feathers" and works of nonfiction, to use that odd term (like calling poetry non-prose) such as Annie Dillard's *Holy the Firm* and Geoffrey Wolff's *The Duke of Deception* and Robert Capon's *The Supper of the Lamb* or plays like *Death of a Salesman* or *Our Town*.

My feeling is that works like those, to name just the few that happen to occur to me first, and all of them written in blood, bring about transfusions that can save souls if not lives. They make good things happen not just in the people who read them but in the very air we breathe. There are lots of other kinds of profound, entertaining, informative books that make lots of other kinds of things happen, but the older I get, the more I find that the ones I am drawn to as a reader and the only ones that I am interested in trying my hand at as a writer are the ones that one way or another make healing and human things happen in a world that is starving for precisely those things, whether it knows that is what it is starving for or not.

A few years ago Alfred Kazin wrote a *New York Times* Sunday book section review of the new edition of *The Oxford Companion to American Literature*. It was a long review, and somewhere toward the middle of it I came across a sentence which read like this: "An eyebrow may be raised here and there at so much space devoted to Frederick Buechner."

Needless to say it stopped me dead in my tracks, and I have thought about those raised eyebrows from time to time ever since. I have never gotten around to comparing the amount of space devoted to me with the amount devoted to other writers of more or less the same general qualifications so I don't know how matters actually stand on that score—I picture naughty little boys measuring each other out behind the barn—but my suspicion is that the real issue the review raised was not how much space I got but that I got any space at all. Generally speaking, my literary credentials are respectable enough, so my guess is that those eyebrows Mr. Kazin mentioned, and for all I know even Mr. Kazin's own eyebrows, were raised on different grounds. I may be wrong, but I think the people who raised them did so because they know that I am an ordained minister and because for that reason they believe that I belong not in an *Oxford Companion to American Literature* but an *Oxford Companion to Religious Propaganda*. I would bet a nickel that if in a moment of madness Andre Dubus or Anne Tyler were to get themselves ordained, the same eyebrows would shoot up all over the place about them.

There are people who are suspicious of writers like me, ordained or otherwise, and unfortunately for us those people are apt to be the movers and shakers of the literary world. They are suspicious of us as pleaders of special causes and promoters of particular points of view. The primacy I have just finished giving to books that make healing and human things happen would be just the kind of evidence they would point to. I think they are suspicious of me in particular because as a writer I am trying to proclaim as convincingly, and at the same time as honestly, as I can the most interesting thing I have found in the world as I have experienced it over the last sixty-four years or so, and that is what I might best call the elusive presence of God among us. I try not to stack the deck or load the dice in my novels. I try to be as true to my experience of the dark and despairing side of things as to the holy and hopeful, but that elusive presence is my continual subject, and of course it raises suspicions and eyebrows all over the place.

I in turn am, if not exactly suspicious of, then at least left cold by, inclined to raise an eyebrow at, writers who are not really interested in proclaiming anything much at all. With a few happy exceptions, I am suspicious of writers whose books end up by the millions in the paperback sections of drug stores and supermarkets and B. Daltons throughout the universe because my guess is that they have written not what they believe is true but only what they believe will wash.

The writers, on the other hand, who get my personal award, are the ones who show exceptional promise of looking at their lives in this world as candidly and searchingly and feelingly and truly as they know how and then of telling the rest of us what they have found there most worth finding. We need the eyes of writers like that to see through. We need the blood of writers like that in our veins.

7

Adolescence and the Stewardship of Pain

All the dictionaries agree that the word adolescent derives from the Latin verb *adolescere*, which is made up of *ad*, meaning toward, and *alescere*, meaning to grow. The word designates human beings who are in the process of growing up. It is as simple as that. Adolescents are the ones who are on their way to becoming what we call adults, from the past participle of *adolescere*: adults, in other words, as the having-grown-up ones, the ones who have the messy and complicated process behind them. Adolescents, that is to say, are on their way to becoming what adults by definition already are.

What I like about that etymology is that it gets us away from the sense of adolescent as a pejorative—don't be so adolescent, we say, or that is a very adolescent way of looking at things—and makes it a purely clinical term. As larva becomes pupa becomes adult in the insect world, so child becomes adolescent becomes adult or grown-up in the human world. It is healthy to be reminded that we are as much a part of the natural order of things as the caterpillar. It is reassuring to be told that for all the mysteries and ambiguities of the human condition, we can at a certain level be as clearly categorized as the common housefly.

What I don't like about it, of course, is that it makes everything sound too tidy. We are as much a part of the animal kingdom as any other animal, but we are also more mysterious and ambiguous than the rest of them, or at least that is the way we experience ourselves. Maybe the process of growing up is no messier or more complicated for us than it is for the dung beetle, but it feels messier and more complicated. Physiologically we leave adolescence behind for adulthood. We look like adults. We sound like adults. We move around through the world more or less like adults. But is the process as comprehensive as the Latin term indicates? Have we joined the ranks of the having-grown-up as conclusively as the past participle suggests? Have we put our growing up behind us as the butterfly puts behind the cocoon? Physiologically yes. Intellectually maybe. But how about psychologically, emotionally? How about sexually? How about spiritually? I will not try to answer for anybody else, but I have no hesitation about answering for myself.

Let me put it this way. My technical adolescence is about half a century behind me, and the youngest of my three children is twenty-five, so that for me their adolescence is mostly a memory too. I taught at Lawrenceville for five years and at Phillips Exeter for nine, so that for a significant time I remained in fairly close touch with the adolescent world well after my own official exit from it. But I haven't taught in a secondary school since 1967, which is also a long time ago. In other words, I have no qualifications for speaking about adolescence with anything like authority except in one respect. I am sixty-four years old. I have fathered children. I have written books. I have letters after my name and an ecclesiastical title before it. I can get into movies and motels at a reduced rate. But to call me an adult or grown-up is an oversimplification at best and a downright misnomer at worst. I am not a past participle but a present participle, even a dangling participle. I am not a having-grown-up one but a growing-up one, a groping-up one, not even sure much of the time just where my growing and groping are taking me or where they are supposed to be taking me. I am a verbal adjective in search of a noun to latch onto, a grower in search of a self to grow into. As far as the outer world is concerned, my acne cleared up around 1945, but in terms of my inner world, it is still with me to add to my general embarrassment and confusion about myself. I speak about adolescence with authority because in many ways I still am in the throes of it. That is my only qualification for addressing myself to the subject here. I am a hybrid, an adult adolescent to whom neither term alone does full justice. So much for the official etymology—useful up to a point and then to be laid aside, at least for me.

Let me put forth an alternate etymology—entirely spurious but my own. It has no basis in linguistic fact but seems truer to the essence of my own experience of adolescence than the official etymology. Let me suggest with total inaccuracy that the word adolescent is made up of the Latin preposition *ad*, meaning toward, and the Latin noun *dolor*, meaning pain. Thus adolescent becomes a term which designates human beings who are in above all else a *painful* process, more specifically those who are in the process of discovering pain itself, of trying somehow to come to terms with pain, to figure out how to deal with pain, not just how to survive pain but how to turn it to some human and creative use in their own encounters with it. Thus adolescents, as in the official etymology, are ones who are growing to be sure but who, in terms of my spurious etymology, are growing in this one specific area of human experience. Adolescents are Adam and Eve in the process of tasting the forbidden fruit and discovering that in addition to good, there is also evil, that in addition to the joy of being alive, there is also the sadness and hurt of being alive and being themselves. Adolescents are Gautama the Buddha as he recognizes the first of the Four Noble Truths, which is that life is suffering, that at any given moment life can be lots of happy things too, but that suffering is universal and inevitable and that to face that reality and to come to terms with that reality is the beginning of wisdom and at the heart of what human growing is all about.

There is no denying that pre-adolescent children know pain too. Abused children, abandoned children, starving or sick children, children who one way or another suffer at home or at school—the newspapers are full of horrors, and I doubt there is one of us who cannot point to the pain of our own childhoods. But remembering myself as a child, I believe that at that early stage of our lives, we have a kind of natural immunity not to the painfulness of what is happening certainly but to the realization that by its nature life itself is painful. The little boy is beaten up by the school bully. The little girl sees her kitten run over. The mother dies. But by the time the next day comes around or the next week, children seem somehow to have been able to cast it off. Psychiatry tells us that maybe the place they cast it is a place deep inside themselves where it will cause them all kinds of trouble in years to come, but at least for as long as the years of childhood last, it is as if it has gone away for good, and the battered child sits in front of the TV screen with a bag of popcorn in her lap as self-forgetful and enraptured by what she sees as if one of the eyes she sees it with is not bruised and swollen from where her father whaled her. Children seem to come into the world with a capacity for living a day at a time. A bad day comes. Then maybe a day that is not so bad or even a good day. Then maybe a bad one again. But by and large children do not seem to keep score. Adolescence, as I etymologize the term, starts when score-keeping starts.

In a novel that I wrote close to twenty years ago, I described the following brief scene based on an incident that took place during my days as teacher at Lawrenceville in the 1950s. It is the teacher himself who is the narrator, a young man named Antonio Parr:

> . . . I remember going on at excessive length to a group of
> ninth graders about what *irony* meant. I think most of them
> understood it well enough before I started, but just to keep
> the silence at bay I rattled on about it anyway. I talked
> about outer meaning and inner meaning. I said that an
> ironic statement was a statement where you said one thing
> but to people who had their ears open said another. I
> explained that when Mark Antony in his funeral oration
> called the Romans who had murdered Caesar honorable
> men, he was being ironic because his inner meaning was
> that they were a bunch of hoods, and when that remark
> didn't seem to get anything started, I waded in deeper still.
> I said that in addition to ironic statements, you also had
> ironic situations. Their silence deepened. I remember then

a small, fat boy named Stephen Kulak. He was young for
the ninth grade and looked it with a round, pink face and
the judicious gaze of a child. He said he saw how something you said could mean two things, but he didn't see
how something that happened could, so I reached down
into my own silence and pulled out the first example that
came to hand. I said suppose you had a bride on her wedding day. Suppose she was all dressed up in her white dress
and wedding veil, and then on her way to the church a car
ran into her and she was killed. That was an ironic situation, I said. It was ironic because on the same day that she
was starting out on a new life, her life stopped. Two things.
Now did he see what ironic meant? I remember watching
him as he sat there at his desk in a Red Baron sweat-shirt
trying to puzzle through my lugubrious illustration until
finally in some dim and memorable way his pink face
seemed to change and he said, "I get it now. It's a kind of
joke," and I could see that he really had gotten it, that there
in a classroom with the Pledge of Allegiance framed on the
wall and Christmas wreaths made of red and green construction paper Scotch-taped to the window panes,
Stephen Kulak had learned from kindly old Mr. Parr, who
had a hard time keeping his mouth shut, what irony was,
and jokes, and life itself if you made the mistake of keeping
your ears open. Once you get the reading and writing out
of the way, I suppose what you teach children in an English
class is, God help you, yourself.*

Much as I remember doing myself, Antonio Parr, the
narrator, feels guilty about having been the one to teach the

---

*Frederick Buechner, *The Book of Bebb* (New York: Atheneum, 1979;
papercover, San Francisco: HarperCollins, 1990), p. 313.

little boy the first of the Buddha's Four Noble Truths, but he might have drawn comfort from the knowledge that life itself would have taught it to him soon enough anyway and maybe not so gently. Maybe the teacher's main business is to teach gently the inevitability of pain. Themselves adolescents in my sense of the word—scorekeepers of *dolor*—maybe teachers have no higher calling than to help the Stephen Kulaks who come their way not just to see what the score is—forewarned is forearmed—but to help them also to see pain as value, the possibility of their pain's becoming one of their richest treasures.

As the Chorus in Shakespeare's *Henry V* puts it, describing the eve of the battle of Agincourt, "Now entertain conjecture of a time / When creeping murmurs and the poring dark / Fills the wide vessel of the universe." Let us instead entertain conjecture of the murmuring dark of a more obscure but in its way no less momentous battle. The place is the house, that corner of the wide vessel of the universe, where at the age of eight or nine I lived with my parents and younger brother. Money was short as it was in many families in those days. My father was drinking too much though in every other way he was a conscientious, caring young man, handsome and full of charm, who over the years had kept changing jobs in the effort to do better by his wife and two small sons. My mother was a beautiful, demanding, discontented young woman who was in many ways a good mother but in most ways not a very good wife.

After a good deal of drinking one evening, my father decided to take the car and go driving off with it somewhere. My mother told him that he was in no condition to drive and wouldn't let him have the keys. I had already gone to bed, and she came upstairs to give the keys to me. She told me that under no circumstances was I to let my father have them. Somehow or other my father found out that I had them—I can only assume that she told him—and came upstairs to ask me to give them to him. He sat down on one twin bed, and I was lying on the one next to it with the covers over my head and the keys in my hand under the pillow. For what seemed an endless time, he sat there pleading with me to let him have them, and I lay there under the covers not saying anything because I no more knew what to say than I knew what to do or to be. I believe that at one point my mother came into the room where we were and excoriated him for humiliating himself in front of his own son. I don't remember how the little domestic Agincourt ended, but I think I finally just went to sleep with the sound of my father's pleading in my ears and the keys, which I never gave him, still clenched tight in my fist under the pillow. The child that I was certainly felt the pain of it as attested to by the fact that I have so long remembered it, but at the time, with the resilience of a child, I simply cast it off together with many other painful scenes like it. Bad days happened and good days happened, and with the capacity of a child for letting life run off me like water off a duck's back, I took them as they came. I lived in the garden where the tree of the knowledge of good and evil grew, but I hadn't yet tasted it.

It wasn't until I was some fifty years deep into my adolescence that I described the scene in a short autobiographical novel called *The Wizard's Tide,* and one day a couple of summers ago I read those few pages out loud to a group of some sixty people or so at a religious retreat in western Texas. I could see that they were moved by it as I read it not because I had written it with any particular eloquence but because, as best I could, I had written it in the simple language of a child in a way that must have awakened in them similar painful memories of their own childhoods. When I finished reading, a man named Howard Butt came up and said a few words to me that opened my eyes to something I had never clearly seen before. He said, "You have had a good deal of pain in your life, and you have been a good steward of it."

I did not hear his words as a compliment although I suppose that is the way he meant them. I could take no credit for being a good steward of my pain—whatever that might mean—because I had had no idea that that was what I was being and had had no intention of being it. But his words caught me off guard and have haunted me ever since. I had always thought of stewardship as a rather boring, churchy word that the minister trots out on Budget Sunday or when launching the Every Member Canvass. I knew that a steward is a caretaker of some kind or other, the person who takes care of, takes care with, money particularly, or real estate, or the stateroom of an ocean liner. But what did it mean to take care of, take care with, the hurtful things that happen to you? How do you go about being the steward of, of all things, your pain?

Suffering is the undercurrent and bedrock of life, the Buddha said. Life is adventure and challenge and community. To live is to taste and touch, to smell and see and listen to, the good things of the earth and to rejoice in them. It is to make friends and to be a friend. It is to create. It is to search for God if you are religiously inclined and, if you are not, to search for something in place of God to give meaning and purpose and value to your scattered days. But you become an adolescent at the moment when you begin to understand that what the Buddha meant is that beneath all of this, inextricably woven into the rich fabric of all of this, there are not just the sad things that happen one by one as they do in childhood, but there is sadness itself—the *lachrymae rerum* as Lucretius puts it, the tears of things, the tears that all things can bring to your eyes when you once realize that dissolution and loss are to be the end of all of them, including the happiest. Adolescents are the ones who, whether fourteen years old or sixty-four years old, are in the process of growing into that knowledge and, if they are ever to become more or less grown-up human beings at last, growing by means of it.

There are many ways of dealing with your pain, and perhaps the most tempting of them all is to forget about it, to hide it not just from the world but also from yourself. It is the way of the stoic, the stiff upper lip. It is the way that is characteristic maybe especially of white Anglo-Saxon Protestants, WASPs, who are taught from infancy that they are to keep their troubles to themselves and that the eighth deadly sin, and one of the deadliest, is self-pity: that it is perfectly proper to pity other people when sorrow strikes, but when you yourself are stricken, you are supposed to keep it under your hat. When the father drinks too much. When the mother in desperation turns into a terrible-tongued shrew. When the child lives in terror. When the marriage comes apart or the business fails or the exam is hopelessly flunked, the rule is not to let yourself feel it any more than you can help, not to trust anybody with the truth of how it hurts, and maybe most of all not to talk about it, certainly not outside of the family and eventually not even there, not even to yourself.

To bury your pain is a way of surviving your pain and therefore by no means to be dismissed out of hand. It is a way which I venture to say has at one time or another served and continues to serve all of us well. But it is not a way of growing. It is not a way of moving through adolescence into adulthood. If you manage to put behind you the painful things that happen to you as if they never really happened or didn't really matter all that much when they did, then the deepest and most human things you have in you to become are not apt to happen either. It was not for many years that the small boy with the keys in his fist came to understand something of the Agincourt that he and his parents and kid brother had long ago all been involved in, with all the chances there might have been for them to be brave, to be kind, to be wise, to be a family; maybe even, on the far side of the murmuring dark of anger and tears, to be reconciled and healed.

The alternative to ignoring your pain is of course to be trapped in it. One thinks of Miss Havisham in Dickens's *Great Expectations* jilted by her lover and living the rest of her life in a darkened room with the wedding dress she was never married in turning to rags upon her and the wedding cake moldering uneaten among the cobwebs. Caricature as she is, she can stand for all those whose pain somewhere along the line stops them dead in their tracks, leaving them to feed endlessly on their own bitterness in a world of enemies none of whom is as deadly as they are to themselves. Or, turning again to Dickens, we find the professional widow Mrs.

Gummidge in *David Copperfield* sniveling into her old black silk handkerchief and croaking her endless dirge of "I'm a lone lorn creetur'" as the one way she thinks she has of winning attention and sympathy because after years of wallowing in her pain she believes she has no other way of winning it. We don't need Dickens to caricature the way we can all of us use pain also as an excuse for failure. If only the terrible thing hadn't happened—the unhappy childhood, the weak heart, the financial disaster—there's no telling what wonderful things we could have done with our lives. In such ways as these, and more, we do the best we can with the worst that happens to us, and insofar as such ways keep the worst from destroying us, there is no denying their usefulness. But although they may help us to survive, they do not help us to grow, to change, to be transformed into something more nearly approaching full personhood. Like the princess in the fairy tale, we take the straw we are given and thatch the roof with it to keep the weather out, but we do not do what we might do which is to spin it into gold.

What does it mean to be a *steward* of your pain as Howard Butt put it? It is at least one of the subjects that I think Jesus himself is talking about in one of the strangest and in a way darkest of the parables he told—strange because it turns out so differently from the way we would have supposed and dark because there is a note of such apparent harshness and unfairness in it. According to the Gospel of Matthew, he told it as follows:

> For it will be as when a man going on a journey called his servants and entrusted to them his property; to one he gave five talents, to another two, to another one, to each accord-

ing to his ability. Then he went away. He who had received the five talents went at once and traded with them; and he made five talents more. So also, he who had the two talents made two talents more. But he who had received the one talent went and dug in the ground and hid his master's money. Now after a long time the master of those servants came and settled accounts with them. And he who had received the five talents came forward, bringing five talents more, saying, "Master, you delivered to me five talents; here I have made five talents more." His master said to him, "Well done, good and faithful servant; you have been faithful over a little, I will set you over much; enter into the joy of your master." And he also who had the two talents came forward saying, "Master, you delivered to me two talents; here I have made two talents more." His master said to him, "Well done, good and faithful servant; you have been faithful over a little, I will set you over much; enter into the joy of your master." He also who had received the one talent came forward, saying, "Master, I knew you to be a hard man, reaping where you did not sow, and gathering where you did not winnow; so I was afraid, and I went and hid your talent in the ground. Here you have what is yours." But his master answered him, "You wicked and slothful servant! You knew that I reap where I have not sowed, and gather where I have not winnowed? Then you ought to have invested my money with the bankers, and at my coming I should have received what was my own with interest. So take the talent from him, and give it to him who has the ten talents. For to every one who has will more be given, and he will have abundance; but from him who has not, even what he has will be taken away. And cast the worthless servant into the outer darkness; there men will weep and gnash their teeth."

Bad times happen, good times happen, life itself happens and happens to all of us in different ways and with different mixtures of good and bad, pain and pleasure, luck and unluck. As I read it, that is what the parable is essentially about, and the question the parable poses is, what do we do with these mixed lives we are given, these hands we are so unequally dealt by God if we believe in God or by circumstance or by our genes or by whatever you want to interpret the rich man as representing? To use the mercenary terms of the parable itself, how do we get the most out of what we are so variously and richly and hair-raisingly given? It is the pain we are given that interests me most here and that I suspect must have interested Jesus too because God knows he was dealt plenty of it himself during his thirty years on this planet, give or take. Two of the servants do one thing with it, and the third servant does something very different with it and with radically different results. What happened to the third servant, of course, is where the harshness and darkness come in.

The third servant takes what he is given—for our purposes let us focus particularly on the pain he is given—and buries it. He takes it and hides it in a hole in the ground and thereby, I would suggest, becomes the blood brother and soul-mate of virtually all of us at one time or another. The small boy buries his hand under the pillow. Miss Havisham buries herself in the darkened room. Mrs. Gummidge buries her face in her black lace handkerchief. We bury for years the tragic memory, the secret fear, the unspoken loneliness, the unspeakable desire. "I was afraid," is what the third servant says when the rich man confronts him years later, and he had good reason to be. We all of us have good reason to be afraid because life is scary as Hell, and I do not use that term lightly. "I knew you to be a hard man," the servant says, "reaping where you did not sow and gathering where you did not winnow," and he is speaking no more or less than the truth. God is hard as well as merciful. Life is hard as well as marvelous. Hard and terrible things happen to us in this world which call us to be strong and brave and wise, to be heroes, when it is all we can do just to keep our heads above water. So we dig the hole in the ground, in ourselves, in our busyness or wherever else we dig it, and hide the terrible things in it, which is another way of saying that we hide ourselves from the terrible things. It seems as unfair to blame us for doing it as it seems unfair to blame the third servant because it is a way of keeping afloat, of saving ourselves from drowning, and yet the words of the parable are devastating. "Wicked and slothful" is what the rich man calls the third servant, who in so many ways can stand for us all—wicked in burying what he should have held to the light and made something of; slothful because playing it safe is another way of not really playing it at all. And then the rich man takes away what little the servant was given in the first place and says he is to be cast "into the outer darkness where men wail and gnash their teeth." It is an extraordinary story to come from the one who has been called the Light of the World and Prince of Peace.

I think that what the parable means is that the buried pain in particular and all the other things we tend to bury along with pain, including joy, which tends to get buried too when we start burying things, that the buried life is itself darkness and wailing and gnashing of teeth and the one who casts us into it is no one other than ourselves. To bury your life is to stop growing, as for years a deep part of the small boy with his hand under the pillow stopped growing and the two old women out of Dickens with him. To bury your life is to have it wither in the ground and diminish. It is to be deeply alone. It is to be less alive than you were to start with. That may sound harsh and dark and unfair, but it is the way things are. It is the truth.

The other two servants are the ones, according to the parable, who get it right and do what they should do with what they have been given. The rich man calls them "good and faithful servants," and what he means apparently is that their goodness *is* their faithfulness—their faith in him, in life itself, which enables them to take it as it comes, the pain of it with the rest of it, and instead of burying it, to live it fully with the faith that one way or another it will work out. Taking the various sums of money they had been given, they "went and traded with them," as the parable puts it, and the word *trade* seems to me the key to what Jesus is saying about them.

To trade is to give of what it is that we have in return for what it is that we need, and what we have is essentially what we are, and what we need is essentially each other. The good and faithful servants were not life-buriers. They were life-traders. They did not close themselves off in fear but opened themselves up in risk and hope. The trading of joy comes naturally because it is of the nature of joy to proclaim and share itself. Joy cannot contain itself, as we say. It overflows. And so it should properly be with pain as well, the parable seems to suggest. We are never more alive to life than when it hurts—never more aware both of our own powerlessness to save ourselves and of at least the possibility of a power beyond ourselves to save us and heal us if we can only open ourselves to it. We are never more aware of our need for each other, never more in reach of each other if we can only bring ourselves to reach out and let ourselves be reached. If only the small boy had been able to say, "I am scared." If only the father had been able to say to the small boy, "I am scared too. I am lost." We are never more in touch with life than when life is painful, never more in touch with hope than we are then, if only the hope of another human presence to be with us and for us.

Being a good steward of your pain involves all those things, I think. It involves being alive to your life. It involves taking the risk of being open, of reaching out, of keeping in touch with the pain as well as the joy of what happens because at no time more than at a painful time do we live out of the depths of who we are instead of out of the shallows. There is no guarantee that we will find a pearl in the depths, that the end of our pain will have a happy end, or even any end at all, but at least we stand a chance of finding in those depths who we most deeply and humanly are and who each other are. At least we stand a chance of finding that we needn't live alone in our pain like Miss Havisham in her darkened room because perhaps more than anything else, the universal experience of pain is what makes us all the brothers and sisters, the parents and children, of each other, and the story of one of us is the story of all of us. And that in itself is a pearl of great price. It is a way of transmuting passion into compassion, of leaving the prison of selfhood for a landscape of selves, of spinning straw into gold. Howard Butt said that I had been a good steward of my pain because I had written a book about it which had moved him and in some measure opened him healingly to depths of his own as the writing of it had opened me to a new dimension of mine. But you do not have to write books about your pain to be a good steward of it. The trouble with writing books about it is that you risk reducing it to just a book you have written. You do not have to go around talking about it. What is perhaps most precious about pain is that if it doesn't destroy us, it can confer on us a humanity that needs no words to tell of it and that can help others become human even as they can help us.

I think of adolescents in the ordinary sense of human beings in the process of growing up. I think particularly of the young men and young women who come to schools like this one and other schools not like this one at all. I think of what we teach them and how we teach them and to what end. Basically, I suppose, what we teach them is how to deal with the world. We teach them history so that they will know where the world is coming from and science so they will know what the world is made of and how it works. We teach them languages, including their own language, so they will be able to communicate successfully with the world and understand what the world is saying when it communicates with them. We give them physical education to develop their sense of what the disciplined human body is capable of and teach them sports to increase their ability to excel and win or, if they must lose, how to lose with grace. Ideally, we teach them something at least about the arts and maybe even about world religions so they will have some familiarity with the dreams the world has dreamed of the great intangibles of truth, beauty, holiness. Less directly than indirectly, less through books than through example, we teach them also, we hope, about certain moral values that will serve them in good stead as they make their way in the world, values like honesty, integrity, industry, prudence, self-confidence, courage, independence. In other words, the essence, I think, of what we teach them is control and competence. We say in effect that this is the world and these are the things that it is important to know in order to live controlled and competent lives in it. We teach these things for the students' sake and also, of course, for the world's sake. If the world is not to succumb to the chaos that continually threatens it, these are things that the young must know.

But I believe there is something else they should know and that as teachers we should know too. The biblical theologian Walter Brueggeman says it as well as anybody I have come across and says it in a short passage where he is speaking specifically about church education but in my view could just as well be speaking about education in general.

> If you ask almost any adult about the impact of church school on his or her growth, he or she will not tell you about books or curriculum or Bible stories or anything like that. The central memory is of the teacher, learning is *meeting*. That poses problems for the characteristically American way of thinking about education for competence even in the church. Meeting never made anybody competent. Surely we need competence, unless we mean to dismantle much of our made world. But our business is not competence. It is meeting. We are learning slowly and late that *education for competence* without *education as meeting* promises us deadly values and scary options. And anyway, one can't become "competent" in morality or in Bible stories. But one can have life-changing meetings that open one to new kinds of existence. And that surely is what church educa-

tion must be about. . . . Our penchant for control and pre-
dictability, our commitment to quantity, our pursuit of
stability and security—all this gives us a sense of priority
and an agenda that is concerned to reduce the element of
surprise and newness in our lives. And when newness and
surprise fail, there is not likely to be graciousness, healing,
or joy. Enough critics have made the point that when expe-
riences of surprise and newness are silenced in our lives,
there is no amazement, and where there is no amazement,
there cannot be the full coming to health, wholeness, and
maturity.*

Education is meeting, Brueggeman says. Living right is trading with what you have been given, Jesus says in his parable.
It is living out of your humanness in a way to call forth the
humanness of the people with whom you are living and your
own humanness. That is what trading and meeting both
point to, and the amazing result can be that new life happens
for you both—as Brueggeman puts it, new graciousness,
healing, or joy. I have concentrated here on the pain that our
humanness inevitably involves because I believe that is the
experience which we are most apt less to trade with than to
bury. It is not just the Buddha who reminds us of that
inevitability but Jesus too if I hear him right; and when he
says, "Come unto me, all you who labor and are heavy laden,"
I believe he is speaking to all of us. The young are no less
heavy laden than the old, the lucky no less than the unlucky,
the young woman in French heels teetering across the platform to receive her diploma no less than the old man watch-

*Walter Brueggeman, *Living Toward a Vision* (New York: United Church
Press, 1987), pp. 167–71.

ing TV in a nursing home. Life is not for sissies no matter
who you are or where or how you are living it. I have con-
jured up a fake etymology that makes *adolescent* mean not just
growing but growing particularly into the experience of pain
and growing by means of that experience. I have spoken of
coming out from under the covers and unclenching the fist
that holds the keys. I have spoken of opening, and reaching
out of, and keeping in touch with your pain because that is
the way it can become one of the richest of your treasures.
But humanness involves joy as well as pain, and it is of
course that experience too that we are bidden to live out of
and to trade with and to meet on the ground of if we are to
be good stewards not just of our most hurtful times but of
our most blessed times as well.

I don't know what all this means, practically speaking,
for educators, but I suspect it means less a change in cur-
riculum or basic pedagogic technique—though both of
these may be involved—than maybe just a small but significant change of heart. I think it means that although distinc-
tions cannot be denied, teacher and student, preacher and
congregation, parent and child, do well not to stand always
at the distance from each other which those terms suggest
but, as often as they can, to meet on the ground of their
common aliveness where each has much to learn not just
from the other but from whatever you call the mystery that
life itself comes from. I don't think that it is always necessary to talk *about* the deepest and most private dimension of
who we are, but I think we are called to talk to each other *out
of* it, and just as importantly to listen to each other out of it,
to live out of our depths as well as our shallows. We are all
of us adolescents, painfully growing and groping our way

toward something like true adulthood, and maybe the greatest value we have both to teach and to learn as we go is the value of what Walter Brueggeman calls amazement—the capacity to be amazed at the unending power that can be generated by the meeting and trading of lives, which is a power to heal us and bless us and in the end maybe even to transform us into truly *human* beings at last.

8

Advice to the Next Generation
(in answer to a question)

I have never been much good at either taking advice (much too proud) or giving it (much too humble). Let me instead then just *mention* to the next generation something which, if somebody had mentioned it to me in the 1940s, when my generation was in line for take-off, might have saved me years of grief and confusion.

My father having died early, I was brought up by my mother to believe that I had no right to be happy unless she was happy. If she had ever come right out and said it, I might have been brave enough or smart enough to tell her she was crazy. But of course she would never have dreamed of saying it in so many words, and consequently I never dreamed that in every other way, whether she was conscious of doing so or not, she had said it so powerfully that I swallowed it hook, line, and sinker without knowing that I had swallowed a thing. I grew up believing that there was something shameful about being happy unless not only my mother but more or less everybody else I felt responsible for and beholden to was happy as well. I think a lot of people grow up believing the same thing. It is a preposterous thing to believe. It is dead wrong. That is what I would like to mention to the next generation.

You have every right to be happy no matter what. If other people are unhappy, you do the best you can for them—that is a lot of what all religions are about and a lot of what love is about too—but you do not deny yourself happiness on their account. It does them no real good if you do. On the contrary. The happier you are able to be inside your own skin—happy in the sense of being at peace with yourself, of taking care of yourself, of giving and receiving the best of what it means to be human—the better your chances are of making them a little happier too because there is no condition more contagious. So be happy for other people's sakes as well as for your own sake. And if you believe in God, be happy for God's sake too because that is what God created you to be. It is why, at the Creation itself, according to Job, the morning stars sang together and all the sons of God shouted for joy.

9

The Clown in the Belfry

The Lord is my shepherd; I shall not want. He maketh me to lie down in green pastures: he leadeth me beside the still waters. He restoreth my soul: he leadeth me in the paths of righteousness for his name's sake. Yea, though I walk through the valley of the shadow of death, I will fear no evil: for thou art with me; thy rod and thy staff they comfort me. Thou preparest a table before me in the presence of my enemies: thou anointest my head with oil; my cup runneth over. Surely goodness and mercy shall follow me all the days of my life: and I will dwell in the house of the Lord forever.

—Psalm 23

Happy Birthday! Happy Birthday to this old church that was first organized two hundred years ago day before yesterday with seven members and a pastor who bore the somewhat less than promising name of Increase Graves. Happy Birthday to this old building that has seen many a howling blizzard in its time and many a scorching summer day before the road it stands on ever dreamed of being paved and the air was thick with the dust of horses' hooves and wagon wheels. Happy Birthday to all of you because more than an organization, more than a building, a church is the people who come to it to pray and sing and fidget and dream, to shed a tear or two if some word strikes home, and to try to keep a straight face if the soloist strikes a sour note or somebody's hearing aid starts to buzz. Happy Birthday to all of you who listen to some sermons and doze through other sermons and do all the other things people do that make them a church and make them human.

And Happy Birthday to Jesus too, I guess it's proper to say, because before this is a Congregational church, or Rupert's church, or your church, it is after all *his* church. If it hadn't been for Jesus, who knows what other kind of building might have stood on this spot or what other line of work Increase Graves might have gone into, or where you and I might be today—not just where we might be geographically but where we might be humanly, inside ourselves, if it hadn't been for Jesus and all the things he said and did and all the things people have kept on saying and doing because of him ever since.

What do you do on a birthday? You get together with your friends, of course. You put on your best clothes. You sing songs. You bring offerings. You whoop it up. You do a lot of the same things, in other words, that we're doing here today, and it seems to me that that's just as it should be. But there's one thing I propose to do that is usually not done on birthdays. Just for a moment or two I suggest we set aside our snappers and party hats and give at least one quick look at what it is that we're whooping it up about, what it is that really makes people into a church in the first place.

Since 1786 people have been coming here the way you and I came here today. Men who fought in the American Revolution and the widows of men who never got back from it. Civil War veterans. Two centuries worth of farmers, dairymen, mill workers, an occasional traveler. Old men and old women with most of their lives behind them, and young men and young women with most of their lives ahead of them. People who made a go of it and are remembered still, and people who somehow never left their mark in any way the world noticed and aren't remembered anymore by anybody. Despite the enormous differences between them, all these men and women entered this building just the way you and I entered it a few minutes ago because of one thing they had in common.

What they had in common was that, like us, they believed (or sometimes believed and sometimes didn't believe; or wanted to believe; or liked to think they believed) that the universe, that everything there is, didn't come about by chance but was created by God. Like us they believed, on their best days anyway, that all appearances to the contrary notwithstanding, this God was a God like Jesus, which is to say a God of love. That, I think, is the crux of the matter. In 1786 and 1886 and 1986 and all the years between, that is at the heart of what has made this place a church. That is what all the whooping has been about. In the beginning it was not some vast cosmic explosion that made the heavens and the earth. It was a loving God who did. That is our faith and the faith of all the ones who came before us.

The question is, is it true? If the answer is No, then what we're celebrating today is at best a happy and comforting illusion. If the answer is Yes, then we have something to celebrate that makes even a two-hundredth birthday look pale by comparison.

I don't suppose there is any passage in either the Old Testament or the New that sums up the faith this church was founded on more eloquently and movingly than the Twenty-third Psalm. "The Lord is my shepherd. I shall not want." How many times would you guess those words have been spoken here over the years, especially at dark moments when people needed all the faith they could muster? How many times have we spoken them ourselves, at our own dark moments? But for all their power to bring comfort, do the words hold water? This faith in God that they affirm, is it borne out by our own experience of life on this planet? That is a hard and painful question to raise, but let us honor the occasion by raising it anyway. Does this ancient and beautiful psalm set forth a faith that in the secrecy of our hearts we can still honestly subscribe to? And what exactly is that faith it sets forth? The music of the psalm is so lovely that it's hard sometimes to hear through it to what the psalm is saying.

"God's in his Heaven, all's right with the world," Robert Browning wrote, and the psalm is certainly not saying that any more than you or I can say it either. Whoever wrote it had walked through the valley of the shadow the way one way or another you and I have walked there too. He says so himself. He believed that God was in his Heaven despite the fact that he knew as well as we do that all was far from right with the world. And he believed that God was like a shepherd.

When I think of shepherds, I think of my friend Vernon Beebe who used to keep sheep here in Rupert a few years back. Some of them he gave names to, and some of them he didn't, but he knew them equally well either way. If one of them got lost, he didn't have a moment's peace till he found it again. If one of them got sick or hurt, he would move

Heaven and earth to get it well again. He would feed them out of a bottle when they were newborn lambs if for some reason the mother wasn't around or wouldn't "own" them, as he put it. He always called them in at the end of the day so the wild dogs wouldn't get them. I've seen him wade through snow up to his knees with a bale of hay in each hand to feed them on bitter cold winter evenings, shaking it out and putting it in the manger. I've stood with him in their shed with a forty-watt bulb hanging down from the low ceiling to light up their timid, greedy, foolish, half holy faces as they pushed and butted each other to get at it because if God is like a shepherd, there are more than just a few ways, needless to say, that people like you and me are like sheep. Being timid, greedy, foolish, and half holy is only part of it.

Like sheep we get hungry, and hungry for more than just food. We get thirsty for more than just drink. Our *souls* get hungry and thirsty; in fact it is often that sense of inner emptiness that makes us know we have souls in the first place. There is nothing that the world has to give us, there is nothing that we have to give to each other even, that ever quite fills them. But once in a while that inner emptiness is filled even so. That is part of what the psalm means by saying that God is like a shepherd, I think. It means that, like a shepherd, he feeds us. He feeds that part of us which is hungriest and most in need of feeding.

There is richer, more profitable land in the world certainly than what we have in this small corner of the state of Vermont, but it's hard to believe there is any lovelier land. There are the sloping hillside pastures and meadows we live among—green pastures, then golden pastures, then pastures whiter than white, blue-shadowed. There are still waters—

the looking-glass waters of pasture ponds filled with sky and clouds—and there are waters that aren't still at all but overflow their banks when the melting snow swells them and they go rattling and roaring and chuckling through the woods in a way that makes you understand how human beings must have first learned what music is. Most of the time we forget to notice this place where we live—because we're so used to it, because we get so caught up in whatever our work is, whatever our lives are—but every once and so often maybe we notice and are filled. "He restoreth my soul," is the way the psalm says it. For a little while the scales fall from our eyes and we actually see the beauty and holiness and mystery of the world around us, and then from deeper down even than our hunger, restoring comes, nourishment comes. You can't make it happen. You can't make it last. But it is a glimpse, a whisper. Maybe it is all we can handle.

"I shall not want," the psalm says. Is that true? There are lots of things we go on wanting, go on lacking, whether we believe in God or not. They are not just material things like a new roof or a better paying job, but things like good health, things like happiness for our children, things like being understood and appreciated, like relief from pain, like some measure of inner peace not just for ourselves but for the people we love and for whom we pray. Believers and unbelievers alike we go on wanting plenty our whole lives through. We long for what never seems to come. We pray for what never seems to be clearly given. But when the psalm says "I shall not want," maybe it is speaking the utter truth anyhow. Maybe it means that if we keep our eyes open, if we keep our hearts and lives open, we will at least never be in want of the one thing we want more than anything else.

Maybe it means that whatever else is withheld, the shepherd never withholds himself, and he is what we want more than anything else.

Not at every moment of our lives, Heaven knows, but at certain rare moments of greenness and stillness, we are shepherded by the knowledge that though all is far from right with any world you and I know anything about, all is right deep down. All will be right at last. I suspect that is at least part of what "He leadeth me in the paths of righteousness" is all about. It means righteousness not just in the sense of *doing* right but in the sense of *being* right—being right with God, trusting the deep-down rightness of the life God has created for us and in us, and riding that trust the way a red-tailed hawk rides the currents of the air in this valley where we live. I suspect that the paths of righteousness he leads us in are more than anything else the paths of trust like that and the kind of life that grows out of that trust. I think that is the shelter he calls us to with a bale in either hand when the wind blows bitter and the shadows are dark.

"Yea, though I walk through the valley of the shadow of death, I will fear no evil." The psalm does not pretend that evil and death do not exist. Terrible things happen, and they happen to good people as well as to bad people. Even the paths of righteousness lead through the valley of the shadow. Death lies ahead for all of us, saints and sinners alike, and for all the ones we love. The psalmist doesn't try to explain evil. He doesn't try to minimize evil. He simply says he will not fear evil. For all the power that evil has, it doesn't have the power to make him afraid.

And why? Here at the very center of the psalm comes the very center of the psalmist's faith. Suddenly he stops speaking about God as "he" because you don't speak that way when the person is right there with you. Suddenly he speaks *to* God instead of about him, and he speaks to him as "thou." "I will fear no evil," he says, "for thou art with me." That is the center of faith. Thou. That is where faith comes from.

When somebody takes your hand in the dark, you're not afraid of the dark anymore. The power of dark is a great power, but the power of light is greater still. It is the shepherd of light himself who reaches out a hand, who is Thou to us. Death and dark are not the end. Life and light are the end. It is what the cross means of course. The cross means that out of death came, of all things, birth. Happy Birthday indeed! The birth we are here to celebrate is not just the birth of this old church in this old town but the birth of new life including our own new life—hope coming out of hopelessness, joy coming out of sorrow, comfort and strength coming out of fear. Thanks be to all that the cross means and is, we need never be afraid again. That is the faith that has kept bringing people to this place from Increase Graves's time to our time. That is what has brought me here. Unless I miss my guess, that is what has brought you here.

The psalmist stops speaking of God as a shepherd then. God becomes instead the host at a great feast. He prepares a table for us the way the table of Holy Communion is prepared for us, and "in the presence of our enemies" he prepares it because there is no other place. Our enemies are always present. All the old enemies are always gathered around us everywhere. I mean the enemies that come at us from within—doubt and self-doubt, anxiety, boredom, loneliness, failure, temptation. Let each of us name our special

enemies for ourselves. How well we know them. How long
we have done battle with them and how long we will doubtless have to go on battling. But no matter. The table is prepared. Our cups are filled to running over. We are anointed
with this occasion itself—with the sense it gives us of how
much we need each other, you and I, and how the party
wouldn't be complete without every last one of us; the sense
we have of being not just strangers, acquaintances, friends,
momentarily gathered under the same roof, but fellow pil-
grims traveling the same long and bewildering road in search
of the same far city. It is a rare glimpse that we catch at this
enchanted table. The feast that is laid for us here is only a
foretaste of the feast to come. The old enemies will be van-
quished at last. "Surely goodness and mercy will follow us
all the days of our lives," as goodness and mercy have followed us our whole lives through even when we thought
they were farthest from us. "And we will dwell in the house
of the Lord forever," a house that is older than Eden and
dearer than home.

Something like that is the faith this psalm sings. In the
secrecy of our hearts can we say Yes to it? We must each of
us answer for ourselves, of course. Some days it's easier to
say Yes than other days. And even when we say Yes there's
always a No lurking somewhere in the shadows just as when
we say No there's always a Yes. That's the way faith breathes
in and breathes out, I think, the way it stays alive and grows.
But a Birthday is a Yes day if ever there was one. So pick up
the snappers and party hats again. Let the feast continue.
And just one final, festal image to grace it with.

In the year 1831, it seems, this church was repaired and
several new additions were made. One of them was a new

steeple with a bell in it, and once it was set in place and painted, apparently, an extraordinary event took place. "When the steeple was added," Howard Mudgett writes in his history, "one agile Lyman Woodard stood on his head in the belfry with his feet toward heaven."

That's the one and only thing I've been able to find out about Lyman Woodard, whoever he was, but it is enough. I love him for doing what he did. It was a crazy thing to do. It was a risky thing to do. It ran counter to all standards of New England practicality and prudence. It stood the whole idea that you're supposed to be nothing but solemn in church on its head just like Lyman himself standing upside down on his. And it was also a magical and magnificent and Mozartian thing to do.

If the Lord is indeed our shepherd, then everything goes topsy-turvy. Losing becomes finding and crying becomes laughing. The last become first and the weak become strong. Instead of life being done in by death in the end as we always supposed, death is done in finally by life in the end. If the Lord is our host at the great feast, then the sky is the limit.

There is plenty of work to be done down here, God knows. To struggle each day to walk the paths of righteousness is no pushover, and struggle we must because just as we are fed like sheep in green pastures, we must also feed his sheep, which are each other. Jesus, our shepherd, tells us that. We must help bear each other's burdens. We must pray for each other. We must nourish each other, weep with each other, rejoice with each other. Sometimes we must just learn to let each other alone. In short, we must love each other. We must never forget that. But let us never forget Lyman Woodard either silhouetted up there against the blue Rupert sky. Let us join him in the belfry with our feet toward Heaven like his because Heaven is where we are heading. That is our faith and what better image of faith could there be? It is a little crazy. It is a little risky. It sets many a level head wagging. And it is also our richest treasure and the source of our deepest joy and highest hope.

IO

Light and Dark

There shall come forth a shoot from the stump of Jesse, and a branch shall grow out of his roots. And the Spirit of the Lord shall rest upon him, the spirit of wisdom and understanding, the spirit of counsel and might, the spirit of knowledge and the fear of the Lord. And his delight shall be in the fear of the Lord. He shall not judge by what his eyes see, or decide by what his ears hear; but with righteousness he shall judge the poor, and decide with equity for the meek of the earth; and he shall smite the earth with the rod of his mouth, and with the breath of his lips he shall slay the wicked. Righteousness shall be the girdle of his waist, and faithfulness the girdle of his loins. The wolf shall dwell with the lamb, and the leopard shall lie down with the kid, and the calf and the lion and the fatling together, and a little child shall lead them. The cow and the bear shall feed; their young shall lie down together; and the lion shall eat straw like the ox. The sucking child shall play over the hole of the asp, and the weaned child shall put his hand on the adder's den. They shall not hurt or destroy in all my holy mountain, for the earth shall be full of the knowledge of the Lord as the waters cover the sea. In that day the root of Jesse shall stand as an ensign to the peoples; him shall the nations seek, and his dwellings shall be glorious.

—Isaiah 11:1—10

In those days came John the Baptist, preaching in the wilderness of Judea. "Repent, for the kingdom of heaven is at hand." For this is he who was spoken of by the prophet Isaiah when he said, "The voice of one crying in the wilderness: prepare the way of the Lord, make his paths straight." Now John wore a garment of camel's hair, and a leather girdle around his waist; and his food was locusts and wild honey. Then went out to him Jerusalem and all the region about the Jordan, and they were baptized by him in the river Jordan, confessing their sins. But when he saw many of the Pharisees and Sadducees coming for baptism, he said to them, "You brood of vipers! Who warned you to flee from the wrath to come? Bear fruit that befits repentance, and do not presume to say to yourselves, 'We have Abraham as our father,' for I tell you, God is able from these stones to raise up children to Abraham. Even now the axe is laid to the root of the trees, every tree therefore that does not bear good fruit is cut down and thrown into the fire. I baptize you with water for repentance, but he who is coming after me is mightier than I, whose sandals I am not worthy to carry; he will baptize you with the Holy Spirit and with fire. His winnowing fork is in his hand, and he will clear his threshing floor and gather his wheat into the granary, but the chaff he will burn with unquenchable fire."

—*Matthew 3:1–12*

"Give us grace that we may cast away the works of darkness, and put upon us the armor of light, now in the time of this mortal life in which thy son Jesus Christ came to visit us in great humility: that in the last day, when he shall come again in his glorious majesty, to judge both the quick and the dead, we may rise to the life immortal."

That is the collect for today which is both the first
Sunday in Advent and also the first Sunday of your hundredth year as a church. All the paradoxical themes of
Advent are compressed into that handful of words: Christ
coming at Christmas time in great humility and again at the
end of time in glorious majesty—Christ coming as a child
to save us and as a king to judge us—mortal life, immortal
life. They clatter against each other like shutters in the wind
with all their points and counterpoints. They all but deafen
us with their message at one and the same time of sin and
grace, justice and mercy, comfort and challenge. "Cast away
the works of darkness," they say, and put on "the armor of
light." Maybe those are the words that best sum up the para-
dox of who we are and where we are. Somewhere between the
darkness and the light. That is where we are as Christians.
And not just at Advent time, but at all times. Somewhere
between the fact of darkness and the hope of light. That is
who we are.

"Advent" means "coming" of course, and the promise of
Advent is that what is coming is an unimaginable invasion.
The mythology of our age has to do with flying saucers and
invasions from outer space, and that is unimaginable enough.
But what is upon us now is even more so—a close encounter
not of the third kind but of a different kind altogether. An
invasion of *holiness*. That is what Advent is about.

What is coming upon the world is the Light of the
World. It is Christ. That is the comfort of it. The challenge
of it is that it has not come yet. Only the hope for it has
come, only the longing for it. In the meantime we are in the
dark, and the dark, God knows, is also in us. We watch and
wait for a holiness to heal us and hallow us, to liberate us

from the dark. Advent is like the hush in a theater just before the curtain rises. It is like the hazy ring around the winter moon that means the coming of snow which will turn the night to silver. Soon. But for the time being, our time, darkness is where we are.

"Faith is the conviction of things not seen," says the Epistle to the Hebrews, and that means that faith is the creation of darkness. Faith is a way of seeing in the dark. It is what makes the darkness endurable. The language of faith itself is dark and shadowy, full of poetry and symbol. Like the collect with its "armor of light." Like Isaiah with his "the wolf shall dwell with the lamb . . . and the calf and lion and the fatling together, and a little child shall lead them." That is the kind of language faith speaks. The danger is that either we dismiss it as mere fairy tale or we become so caught up by its fairy tale power to enchant us with its beauty that we forget that its whole point as poetry is to point us to its truth.

It points us to ourselves, God knows. Nothing could be clearer or surer than that. We are the wolves and the lambs who even after all this time haven't yet learned how to dwell together in peace. We are the people who walk in darkness as to one degree or another people have always walked in darkness, with the chief difference being that we are the first to have machines of destruction powerful enough to make darkness the end of everything, to leave the surface of the earth as cratered and lifeless as the moon. For years we have tried to believe that the more weapons we have and the more devastating they are, the less likely either we or our enemies will ever be to use them. But even though we have not used them yet, they have brought about a kind of nuclear winter inside us—the way we think about the future, the way we think about ourselves and the nations we consider our enemies, the sense of futility and despair that are part of our inner darkness.

Fear is part of that darkness too, of course. If you are afraid of something long enough, the fear itself can become as destructive as the thing you fear. And blindness is part of it. We know that nothing is worth blowing up the world for. We know that real peace is not just the absence of war but the presence of at least some measure of trust and understanding between nations that for years the Cold War has made impossible. We know that beneath all the differences that divide us from the Russians, we are sisters and brothers even so, and if we can't find a way of living together in our common home which is this planet Earth, we are doomed to die together, their children with our children, our best dreams with their best dreams. If we are Christians, we know that Christ said, "Love your enemies," and if that sounds like a crazy thing to do, who can say that it is any crazier than the arms race.

All these things we know, and know not just as Sunday school truths but as truths borne out by our own deepest experience of ourselves. And yet we live as though we did not know them. Most of the time we live blind to our own best interests let alone to the best interests of anybody else. We live blind to the fact that little by little we are destroying both ourselves and our world. That is the darkness of it.

This is the light. "There shall come forth a shoot from the stump of Jesse, and the Spirit of the Lord shall rest upon him, the Spirit of Wisdom and Understanding . . . righteousness shall be the girdle of his waist and faithfulness shall be the girdle of his loins." Between the fact of darkness and the hope of light, that is where we live. Just the hope alone is like a lamp in the window. Now is "the time of this mortal life in which. . . . Jesus came to visit us in great humility," says the collect. It is the word *visit* that is so moving somehow. He came in the winter as we tell it. He came in the dark and cold. The only light was starlight, not enough to thread a needle by or even read a book. And only for a little while. He visited us. He paid us a visit.

It was thousands of years ago and thousands of miles away, but it is a visit that for all our madness and cynicism and indifference and despair we have never quite forgotten. The oxen in their stalls. The smell of hay. The shepherds standing around. That child and that place are somehow the closest of all close encounters, the one we are closest to, the one that brings us closest to something that cannot be told in any other way. This story that faith tells in the fairy tale language of faith is not just that God *is* which God knows is a lot to swallow in itself much of the time, but that God *comes*. Comes here. "In great humility." There is nothing much humbler than being born: naked, totally helpless, not much bigger than a loaf of bread. But with righteousness and faithfulness the girdle of his loins. And to *us* came. *For* us came. Is it true—not just the way fairy tales are true but as the truest of all truths? Almighty God, are you true?

When you are standing up to your neck in darkness, how do you say Yes to that question? You say Yes, I suppose, the only way faith can ever say it if it is honest with itself. You say Yes with your fingers crossed. You say it with your heart in your mouth. Maybe that way we can say Yes. He visited us. The world has never been quite the same since. It is still a very dark world, in some ways darker than ever before, but the darkness is different because he keeps getting born into it. The threat of holocaust. The threat of poisoning the earth and sea and air. The threat of our own deaths. The broken marriage. The child in pain, the lost chance. Anyone who has ever known him has known him perhaps better in the dark than anywhere else because it is in the dark where he seems to visit most often.

On Christmas morning, as a child, you wake up as early as 4 A.M. maybe, and what sets your heart pounding and keeps you from going back to sleep is the almost unbearable hope that when day finally dawns, you will go downstairs, and there under the tree will be that one gift of all gifts that you have been waiting for for so long that you never believed you would ever get it. We are not children any more and the rubble of the years lies heavy on what was once our capacity for such wonder and excitement as that, but I suspect that deep down inside we go on watching and waiting that way even so. I suspect that maybe the innermost truth about who we are as human beings is that even at our most jaded, even when we're least conscious of it, we wait and watch for the one gift of all gifts still.

The Light of the World. It will come by starlight, by shepherds' light. And it will come also with the light of fire, John the Baptist reminds us in the passage from Matthew. You would expect that fierce, unyielding man to remind us of that fierce, unyielding side of things: that the one who comes to save is the one who comes also to judge. "He will gather wheat into the granary, but the chaff he will burn with unquenchable fire," John says. Is the terrible justice different from the terrible mercy, then? I think not. I think maybe the justice too is part of the great gift, part of the mercy of it—to destroy, for our own sakes, all there is in us that has to be destroyed if we are ever to be saved, if we are ever to become what in our heart of hearts we yearn to be.

Let each of us name for ourselves what there is in us that has to be destroyed. By the unquenchable fire of truth we see our own falseness, of great-heartedness our own pettiness, of true righteousness our own phoniness, our own little complacencies and pieties and hypocrisies. If today is the first day of the rest of our lives, as the saying goes, today is also the last day of this much of our lives, and in the light of the unquenchable fire the past days of each of us are revealed with almost unbearable clarity.

What if anything have you and I done to do battle against the great darkness of things? As parents and the children of our own parents, as wives and husbands and friends and lovers, as players of whatever parts we have chosen to play in this world, as wielders of whatever kind of power, as possessors of whatever kind of wealth, what other human selves have we sacrificed something of our own sweet selves for, in order to help and heal?

"Bear fruit that befits repentance!" thunders the Baptist. "Give us grace that we may cast away the works of darkness and put upon us the armor of light," whispers the prayer we pray. Bear fruit. Put on light like a garment, like a uniform. That is the place to stop and also the place to start. It is the place to stop and *think*—think back, think ahead, think deep. It is the place to start and *be*.

When you invited me to come speak at this anniversary of your founding as a church you had no way of knowing that the minister who founded you, a man named George

Shinn, happened to be my wife's great grandfather, and it pleases me to think that maybe that was not entirely a coincidence. In any case, it was this same George Shinn who in 1880, five years before being asked to start your church here in Chestnut Hill, was summoned once at midnight to the bedside of an old woman who lived by herself without much in the way of either money or friends, and was dying. She managed to convey that she wanted some other woman to come stay with her for such time as she might have left, so George Shinn and the old woman's doctor struck out in the darkness to try to dig one up for her. It sounds like a parable the way it is told, and I am inclined to believe that if someone were ever to tell the story of your lives and mine, they also would sound more like parables than we ordinarily suppose. They knocked at doors and threw pebbles at second story windows. One woman said she couldn't come because she had children. Another said she simply wouldn't know what to do, what to be, in a crisis like that. Another was suspicious of two men prowling around at that hour of night and wouldn't even talk to them. But finally, as the memoir of Dr. Shinn puts it in the prose of another age, "They rapped at the humble door of an Irish woman, the mother of a brood of children. She put her head out of the window. 'Who's there?' she said. 'And what can you want at this time of night?' They tell her the situation, her warm, Irish heart cannot resist. 'Will you come?' 'Sure and I'll come, and I'll do the best I can.' And she did come," the account ends. "She did the best she could."

People like you and me, no less than the Irish woman with sleep in her eyes and her hair in a tangle—the best we *can* is better than the best we *are* because the one who by his coming makes such extraordinary demands of us is the one who by his coming also makes us the extraordinary gift of being able to meet those demands. It is by amazing grace that the light which even the likes of us can sometimes bring to the dark and needful streets where our lives lead us is no less than the Light of the World, which is Christ. Christ is brought to us, and we can bring Christ to each other. That is the mystery of Advent, where justice and mercy, comfort and challenge, the holy and the human, all meet. It is the highest of all adventures.

I I

The Truth of Stories

*Give ear, O my people, to my teaching; incline your ears to
the words of my mouth! I will open my mouth in a parable; I
will utter dark sayings from of old, things that we have heard
and known, that our fathers have told us. We will not hide
them from our children, but tell to the coming generation the
glorious deeds of the Lord and his might, and the wonders
which he has wrought.* —Psalm 78:1–4

*All this Jesus said to the crowd in parables; indeed he said
nothing to them without a parable. This was to fulfill what
was spoken by the prophet: "I will open my mouth in parables, I will utter what has been hidden since the foundation of
the world.* —Matthew 13:34

Somebody should write a book someday about the silences
in Scripture. Maybe somebody already has. "For God alone
my soul waits in silence," the Psalmist says, which is the
silence of waiting. Or "Be not silent, O God of my praise,"
which is the silence of the God we wait for. "And when the
Lamb opened the seventh seal," says the Book of Revelation,
"there was silence in Heaven"—the silence of creation itself

129

coming to an end and of a new creation about to begin. But the silence that has always most haunted me is the silence of Jesus before Pilate. Pilate asks his famous question, "What is truth?" and Jesus answers him with a silence that is almost overwhelming in its eloquence. In case there should be any question as to what that silence meant, on another occasion Jesus put it into words for his disciple Thomas. "I," he said. "I am the truth."

Jesus did not say that religion was the truth or that his own teachings were the truth or that what people taught about him was the truth or that the Bible was the truth or the Church or any system of ethics or theological doctrine. There are individual truths in all of them, we hope and believe, but individual truths were not what Pilate was after or what you and I are after either unless I miss my guess. Truths about this or that are a dime a dozen, including religious truths. THE truth is what Pilate is after: the truth about who we are and who God is if there is a God, the truth about life, the truth about death, the truth about truth itself. That is the truth we are all of us after.

It is a truth that can never be put into words because no words can contain it. It is a truth that can never be caught in any doctrine or creed including our own because it will never stay still long enough but is always moving and shifting like air. It is a truth that is always beckoning us in different ways and coming at us from different directions. And I think that is precisely why whenever Jesus tries to put that ultimate and inexpressible truth into words (instead of into silence as he did with Pilate) the form of words he uses is a form that itself moves and shifts and beckons us in different ways and comes at us from different directions. That is to say he tells stories.

Jesus does not sound like Saint Paul or Thomas Aquinas or John Calvin when we hear him teaching in the Gospels. "Once upon a time" is what he says. Once upon a time somebody went out to plant some seeds. Once upon a time somebody stubbed a toe on a great treasure. Once upon a time somebody lost a precious coin. The Gospels are full of the stories Jesus tells, stories that are alive in somewhat the way the truth is alive, the way he himself is alive when Pilate asks him about truth, and his silence is a way of saying, "Look at my aliveness if you want to know! Listen to my life!" Matthew goes so far as to tell us that "he said nothing to them without a parable," that is to say without a story, and then quotes the words, "I will open my mouth in parables, I will utter what has been hidden since the foundation of the world." In stories the hiddenness and the utterance are both present, and that is another reason why they are a good way of talking about God's truth which is part hidden and part uttered too.

It is too bad we know Jesus' stories so well, or think we do. We have read them so often and heard them expounded in so many sermons that we have all but lost the capacity for hearing them even, let alone for hearing what they are really about. His stories are like photographs that have been exposed to the light so long they have faded almost beyond recognition. They are like family anecdotes so ancient and time-honored we groan at their approach. And what a pity that is when you think what rich stories they are till preachers start making a homiletic shambles of them—so full of surprises and sudden reversals and sad Jewish comedy before people start delivering sermons about them.

The worst of it, of course, is the way we think we know what Jesus' stories mean. Heaven knows people like me who ought to know better have explained the life out of them often enough, have tried so hard to pound the point in that more often than not all you can hear is the pounding. The story about the Good Samaritan, for instance. Is the point of it that our neighbor is anybody who needs us and that loving our neighbor means doing whatever needs to be done even if it costs an arm and a leg to do it? That is a good point as points go, but does getting it mean that now we can move on to the next story? How about the one about the wise women who fill their lamps with oil and the foolish ones who forget to so that when Love himself looms up out of the night with vine leaves in his hair and his eyes aflame, they are left in the dark while the others go in to the marriage supper to have the time of their lives. Having gotten whatever the point of that one is, can we move on again and suck the next one dry?

If we think the purpose of Jesus' stories is essentially to make a point as extractable as the moral at the end of a fable, then the inevitable conclusion is that once you get the point, you can throw the story itself away like the rind of an orange when you have squeezed out the juice. Is that true? How about other people's stories? What is the point of *A Midsummer Night's Dream* or *The Iliad* or *For Whom the Bell Tolls?* Can we extract the point in each case and frame it on the living room wall for our perpetual edification?

Or is the story itself the point and truth of the story? Is the point of Jesus' stories that they point to the truth about you and me and our stories? We are the ones who have been mugged, and we are also the ones who pass by pretending we don't notice. Hard as it is to believe, maybe every once in a while we are even the ones who pay an arm and a leg to help. The truth of the story is not a motto suitable for framing. It is a truth that one way or another, God help us, we live out every day of our lives. It is a truth as complicated and sad as you and I ourselves are complicated and sad, and as joyous and as simple as we are too. The stories that Jesus tells are about us. Once upon a time is *our* time, in other words.

Once upon a time, for instance, I got fed up and left home, got the hell out, no matter why. I bought a one-way ticket for as far as there was to go and got off at the last stop. I spent myself down to where I didn't have the price of a cup of coffee, and that was not the worst of it. The worst of it was I didn't give a damn because there wasn't anything else I wanted even if I'd had the price. There wasn't anything to see I hadn't seen. There wasn't anything to do I hadn't done. There wasn't anything to lose I hadn't lost. The only worse thing than being fed up with the world is being fed up with yourself. I envied the pigs their slops because at least they knew what they were hungry for whereas I was starving to death and had no idea why. All I knew was that the empti-ness inside me was bigger than I was. So I went back. As I might have guessed, the old man was waiting for me. I was ready to crawl to him, say anything he wanted. He looked smaller than I remembered him. He looked small and break-able against the tall sky. His coat didn't look warm enough. It flapped around his shins. We ran the last length between us if you could call the way he did it running. I couldn't get a word out. My mouth was pushed crooked against his chest, he held me so tight. I was blinded by whatever blinded me. I could still hear though. I could hear the thump of his old ticker through the skimpy coat. I could hear his voice break.

Once upon a time again—and as far as I'm concerned, being brother to the one who in his own sweet time came back, it was only right he should hear the breaking of the old man's voice because he was the one who broke it as sure as if he'd taken a stick to it. Yet you'd have thought he was the golden-haired darling of the world the way the old man carried on. More to the point, you'd have thought the old man was senile, pathetic. I have been faithful. I have been dutiful. I have given him the best years of my life and asked nothing in return. And I think he hardly sees me sometimes when he passes me in the field with those watery old eyes. I would sooner gnaw the hand off my wrist than make merry with an ass over the triumphal return of a pig.

Once upon a time, and at this time now, and for as far beyond time as east is beyond west, I that am the ass, laboring under my holy and appalling burden, love them both. I love the pig and I also love the fox, if foxes are the ones that gnaw off their hands. I love them both because the great feast wouldn't be complete without either of them. I love them to the point where if either of them had to suffer some awful pain, I would suffer it in either of their places if that meant they didn't have to. I think I would even be willing to die for them if by some unthinkable chain of events it should ever come down to that.

These stories Jesus tells. Every once in a while it is not just the point that we see but ourselves that we see and each other that we see and God that we see—the whole great landscape of things lit up for a moment as if by lightning on a dark night. And there is more to it than that, of course. Jesus doesn't just tell stories. He himself is a story.

Jesus is the Word made flesh, the truth narrated in bone and bowel, space and time. That is the story he is. He is the one who tells the waves of the sea to stop their raging and throws the money-changers out of the temple in a rage. He is the one who says the only way to make it to the Kingdom of Heaven is to be like little children who don't care beans about making it to the Kingdom of Heaven but just let Heaven happen the way they let everything else happen. He is the one who scandalizes decent people with his eating and drinking and blasphemies, not to mention with the company he keeps, and who weeps when the friend dies he might have saved if only he had been there. He is the one who tells us we must love our enemies and then tells his own enemies that they are vipers and stink of death underneath their whitewash and tells them that exactly *because* he loves them. He is also the one who is hauled up before Pilate looking as if he had been run over by a truck, that part of his story too as it converges briefly with Pilate's story. Pilate wants Jesus to tell him what truth is so he can put it in his pocket and go his way just that much the wiser but otherwise the same old Pilate. But Jesus will not give him the words he wants any more than God would give them to Job when Job wanted them because words are not the point. Jesus himself is the point.

You can hardly blame Pilate for washing his hands of him. He asks so bloody much, this Jesus. Bloody is the word for it. How religious people do treasure all their doctrines and theologies and creeds and catchphrases. How we love moving them around like checkers on a checkerboard just the way Pilate would have loved Jesus to give him some religious truth or another he could play around with and even maybe make his own. But Jesus goes farther than that. What he calls us to is the terrifying game of letting *him* enormously move *us* as the story of him lives and breathes and converges on us beyond all our ideas of him; as it bids us, moves us, to do and to be God only knows what, which can be a very bloody business indeed if we do it right. When we put crosses up in our Protestant churches, we take the body off first as if once the resurrection happens, we somehow no longer have to worry about the crucifixion any more—as if once we have gotten the message of Jesus' life, grasped the point of it (whatever that means), we can set the life itself aside along with the death like the rind of the squeezed orange again. It becomes merely something we can draw on for moral guidance perhaps or spiritual comfort or religious truth.

Only Jesus himself is the truth, the whole story of him. He will not let us settle for any truth less than that, tidier than that, easier than that. And the truth seems to be that if he is indeed everybody's best friend the way the old Jesus hymns proclaim, he is at the same time everybody's worst enemy. He is the enemy, at least, of everything in us that keeps us from giving him what he is really after. And what he is really after is our heart's blood, our treasure, our selves themselves. It is the cross he is inviting us to, not a Sunday school picnic, and therefore if it is proper to rejoice in his presence, it is proper also to be scared stiff in his presence.

He tells us not to be this or to be that, but to be his. Not to follow this way or that way, but to follow him. He promises to give us everything and in return asks us to give up everything the way he himself gave up everything—that is his story. And only then the miracle that not even all our tragic and befuddled history has ever quite managed to destroy. Only then the miracle of you and me not just talking about him two thousand years later but holding on to him for dear life, believing from time to time that he is indeed the one we draw dear life from, dearest life. That is his story too, and of course it is also our story.

So in the long run the stories all overlap and mingle like searchlights in the dark. The stories Jesus tells are part of the story Jesus is, and the other way round. And the story Jesus is is part of the story you and I are because Jesus has become so much a part of the world's story that it is impossible to imagine how any of our stories would have turned out without him, even the stories of people who don't believe in him or even know who he is or care about knowing. And my story and your story are all part of each other too if only because we have sung together and prayed together and seen each other's faces so that we are at least a footnote at the bottom of each other's stories.

In other words all our stories are in the end one story, one vast story about being human, being together, being here. Does the story point beyond itself? Does it mean something? What is the truth of this interminable, sprawling story we all of us are? Or is it as absurd to ask about the truth of it as it is to ask about the truth of the wind howling through a crack under the door?

Either life is holy with meaning, or life doesn't mean a damn thing. You pay your money and you take your choice.

Only never take your choice too easily, of course. Never assume that because you have taken it one way today, you may not take it another way tomorrow.

One choice is this. It is to choose to believe that the truth of our story is contained in Jesus' story, which is a love story. Jesus' story is the truth about who we are and who the God is who Jesus says loves us. It is the truth about where we are going and how we are going to get there if we get there at all and what we are going to find if we finally do. Only for once let us not betray the richness and depth and mystery of that truth by trying to explain it.

Let us instead tell a story which is the story about every one of us. It is a story about a pig, and a fox, and an ass under his holy and appalling burden. It is a story about a mouth pushed crooked, about a voice breaking. Let the rest be Christ's silence.

12

Growing Up

And Moses went up unto God, and the Lord called unto him out of the mountain, saying, Thus shalt thou say to the house of Jacob, and tell the children of Israel: Ye have seen what I did unto the Egyptians and how I bore you on eagles' wings, and brought you unto myself. Now therefore, if ye will obey my voice indeed, and keep my covenant, then ye shall be a peculiar treasure unto me above all people; for all the earth is mine; and ye shall be unto me a kingdom of priests and an holy nation. These are the words which thou shalt speak unto the children of Israel.   —Exodus 19:3–6

So put away all malice and all guile and insincerity and envy and all slander. Like newborn babes, long for the pure spiritual milk, that by it you may grow up to salvation; for you have tasted the kindness of the Lord. You are a chosen race, a royal priesthood, a holy nation, God's own people, that you may declare the wonderful deeds of him who called you out of darkness into his marvelous light.
—1 Peter 2:1–3, 9

"Rich man, poor man, beggar man, thief, doctor, lawyer, merchant chief," or "Indian chief" sometimes if that is how you happened to be feeling that day. That was how the rhyme went in my time anyway, and you used it when you were counting the cherry pits on your plate or the petals on a daisy or the buttons on your shirt or your blouse. The one you ended up counting was, of course, the one you ended up being: Rich? Poor? Standing on a street corner with a tin cup in your hand? Or maybe a career in organized crime?

What in the world, what in heaven's name, were you going to be when you grew up? It was not just another question. It was the great question. In fact everything I want to say here is based on the belief that it is the great question still. What are you going to be? What am I going to be? I have been in more or less the same trade now for some thirty years and contemplate no immediate change, but I like to think of it still as a question that is wide open. For God's sake, what do you suppose we are going to be, you and I? When we grow up.

Something in us rears back in indignation, of course. We are not children any more, most of us. Surely we have our growing up behind us. We have come many a long mile and thought many a long thought. We have taken on serious responsibilities, made hard decisions, weathered many a crisis. Surely the question is, rather, what are we now and how well are we doing at it? If not doctors, lawyers, merchant chiefs, we are whatever we are—computer analysts, businesswomen, school teachers, artists, ecologists, ministers even. We like to think that one way or another we have already made our mark on the world. So isn't the question not, what are we going to be? but, what are we now? We don't have to count cherry pits to find out what we are going to do with our lives because, for better or worse, those dice have already been cast. Now we simply get on with the game, whatever is left of it for us. That is what life is all about from here on out.

But then. Then maybe we have to listen—listen back farther than the rhymes of our childhood even, thousands of years farther back than that. A thick cloud gathers on the mountain as the book of Exodus describes it. There are flickers of lightning, jagged and dangerous. A clap of thunder shakes the earth and sets the leaves of the trees trembling, sets even you and me trembling a little if we have our wits about us. Suddenly the great *shophar* sounds, the ram's horn—a long-drawn, pulsing note louder than thunder, more dangerous than lightning—and out of the darkness, out of the mystery, out of some cavernous part of who we are, a voice calls: "Now therefore, if ye will obey my voice indeed, and keep my covenant, then ye shall be a peculiar treasure unto me above all people"—my *segullah,* the Hebrew word is, my precious ones, my darlings—"and ye shall be unto me a kingdom of priests and a holy nation."

Then, thousands of years later but still thousands of years ago, there is another voice to listen to. It is the voice of an old man dictating a letter. There is reason to believe that he may actually have been the one who up till almost the end was the best friend that Jesus had: Peter himself. "So put away all malice and all guile and insincerity and envy and all slander," he says. "Like newborn babes, long for the pure spiritual milk that by it you may grow up to salvation; for you have tasted the kindness of the Lord." And then he echoes the great cry out of the thunderclouds with a cry of his own. "You are a chosen race, a royal priesthood, a holy nation, God's own people," he says, "that you may declare the wonderful deeds of him who called you out of darkness into his marvelous light."

What are we going to *be* when we grow up? Not what are we going to *do*, what profession are we going to follow or keep on following, what niche are we going to occupy in the order of things. But what are we going to *be*—inside ourselves and among ourselves? That is the question that God answers with the Torah at Sinai. That is the question that the old saint answers in his letter from Rome.

HOLY. That is what we are going to be if God gets his way with us. It is wildly unreasonable because it makes a shambles out of all our reasonable ambitions to be this or to be that. It is not really a human possibility at all because holiness is Godness and only God makes holiness possible. But being holy is what growing up in the full sense means, Peter suggests. No matter how old we are or how much we have achieved or dream of achieving still, we are not truly grown up until this extraordinary thing happens. Holiness is what is to happen. Out of darkness we are called into "his marvelous light," Peter writes, who knew more about darkness than most of us if you stop to think about it, and had looked into the very face itself of Light. We are called to have faces like that—to be filled with light so that we can be bearers of light. I have seen a few such faces in my day, and so have you, unless I miss my guess. Are we going to be rich, poor, beggars, thieves, or in the case of most of us a little of each? Who knows? In the long run, who even cares? Only one thing is worth really caring about, and it is this: "Ye shall be unto me a kingdom of priests and a holy nation."

Israel herself was never much good at it, God knows. That is what most of the Old Testament is mostly about.

Israel did not want to be a holy nation. Israel wanted to be a nation like all the other nations, a nation like Egypt, like Syria. She wanted clout. She wanted security. She wanted a place in the sun. It was her own way she wanted, not God's way; and when the prophets got after her for it, she got rid of the prophets, and when God's demands seemed too exorbitant, God's promises too remote, she took up with all the other gods who still get our votes and our money and our 9 A.M. to 5 P.M. energies, because they are gods who could not care less whether we are holy or not, and promise absolutely everything we really want and absolutely nothing we really need.

We cannot very well blame Israel because of course we are Israel. Who wants to be holy? The very word has fallen into disrepute—holier-than-thou, holy Joe, holy mess. And "saint" comes to mean plaster saint, somebody of such stifling moral perfection that we would run screaming in the other direction if our paths ever crossed. We are such children, you and I, the way we do such terrible things with such wonderful words. We are such babes in the woods the way we keep getting lost.

And yet we have our moments. Every once in a while, I think, we actually long to be what out of darkness and mystery we are called to be; when we hunger for holiness even so, even if we would never dream of using the word. There come moments, I think, even in the midst of all our cynicism and worldliness and childishness, maybe especially then, when there is something about the saints of the earth that bowls us over a little. I mean real saints. I mean saints as men and women who are made not out of plaster and platitude and moral perfection but out of human flesh. I mean saints who have their rough edges and their blind spots like everybody else but whose lives are transparent to something so extraordinary that every so often it stops us dead in our tracks. Light-bearers. Life-bearers.

I remember once going to see the movie *Gandhi* when it first came out, for instance. We were the usual kind of noisy, restless Saturday night crowd as we sat there waiting for the lights to dim with our popcorn and soda pop, girl friends and boy friends, legs draped over the backs of the empty seats in front of us. But by the time the movie came to a close with the flames of Gandhi's funeral pyre filling the entire wide screen, there was not a sound or a movement in that whole theater, and we filed out of there—teenagers and senior citizens, blacks and whites, swingers and squares—in as deep and telling a silence as I have ever been part of.

"You have tasted of the kindness of the Lord," Peter wrote. We had tasted it. In the life of that little bandy-legged, bespectacled man with his spinning wheel and his bare feet and whatever he had in the way of selfless passion for peace and passionate opposition to every form of violence, we had all of us tasted something that at least for a few moments that Saturday night made every other kind of life seem empty, something that at least for the moment I think every last one of us yearned for the way in a far country you yearn for home.

"Ye shall be unto me a kingdom of priests, a holy nation." Can a nation be holy? It is hard to imagine it. Some element of a nation maybe, some remnant or root—"A shoot coming forth from the stump of Jesse," as Isaiah put it, "that with righteousness shall judge the poor and decide with equity for the meek of the earth." The eighteenth-century men and

women who founded this nation dreamed just such a high
and holy dream for us too and gave their first settlements
over here names to match. New Haven, New Hope, they
called them—names that almost bring tears to your eyes if
you listen to what they are saying, or once said. Providence.
Concord. Salem, which is *shalom*, the peace of God. Dreams
like that die hard, and please God there is still some echo of
them in the air around us. But for years now, the meek of the
earth have been scared stiff at the power we have to blow the
earth to smithereens a thousand times over and at our failure
year after year to work out with our enemies a way of signifi-
cantly limiting that hideous power. In this richest of all
nations, the poor go to bed hungry, if they are lucky enough
to have a bed, because after the staggering amounts we continue to spend on defending ourselves, there is not enough
left over to feed the ones we are defending, to help give them
decent roofs over their heads, decent schools for their children, decent care when they are sick and old.

The nation that once dreamed of being a new hope, a
new haven, for the world, has for years been one of the two
great bullies of the world who have blundered and blustered
their way towards unspeakable horror. Maybe that is the way
it inevitably is with nations. They are so huge and complex.
By definition they are so exclusively concerned with their
own self-interest conceived in the narrowest terms that they
have no eye for holiness, of all things, no ears to hear the
great command to be saints, no heart to break at the
thought of what this world could be—the friends we could
be as nations, the common problems we could help each
other solve, all the human anguish we could join together to
heal.

You and I are the eyes and ears. You and I are the heart. It is to us that Peter's letter is addressed. "So put away all guile and insincerity and envy and all slander," he says. No *shophar* sounds or has to sound. It is as quiet as the scratching of a pen, as familiar as the sight of our own faces in the mirror. We have always known what was wrong with us. The malice in us even at our most civilized. Our insincerity, the masks we do our real business behind. The envy, the way other people's luck can sting like wasps. And all slander, making such caricatures of each other that we treat each other like caricatures, even when we love each other. All this infantile nonsense and ugliness. "Put it away!" Peter says. "Grow up to salvation!" For Christ's sake, grow up.

Grow up? For old people isn't it a little too late? For young people isn't it a little too early? I do not think so. Never too late, never too early, to grow up, to be holy. We have already tasted it after all—tasted the kindness of the Lord, Peter says. That is a haunting thought. I believe you can see it in our eyes sometimes. Just the way you can see something more than animal in animals' eyes, I think you can sometimes see something more than human in human eyes, even yours and mine. I think we belong to holiness even when we cannot believe it exists anywhere let alone in ourselves. That is why everybody left that crowded shopping-mall theater in such unearthly silence. It is why it is hard not to be haunted by that famous photograph of the only things that Gandhi owned at the time of his death: his glasses and his watch, his sandals, a bowl and spoon, a book of songs. What does any of us own to match such riches as that?

Children that we are, even you and I, who have given up so little, know in our hearts not only that it is more blessed to give than to receive but that it is also more fun—the kind of holy fun that wells up like tears in the eyes of saints, the kind of blessed fun in which we lose ourselves and at the same time begin to find ourselves, to grow up into the selves we were created to become.

When Henry James, of all people, was saying goodbye once to his young nephew Billy, his brother William's son, he said something that the boy never forgot. And of all the labyrinthine and impenetrably subtle things that that most labyrinthine and impenetrable old romancer could have said, what he did say was this: "There are three things that are important in human life. The first is to be kind. The second is to be kind. The third is to be kind."

Be kind because although kindness is not by a long shot the same thing as holiness, kindness is one of the doors that holiness enters the world through, enters us through—not just gently kind but sometimes fiercely kind.

Be kind enough to yourselves not just to play it safe with your lives for your own sakes but to spend at least part of your lives like drunken sailors—for God's sake, if you believe in God, for the world's sake, if you believe in the world—and thus to come alive truly.

Be kind enough to others to listen, beneath all the words they speak, for that usually unspoken hunger for holiness which I believe is part of even the unlikeliest of us because by listening to it and cherishing it maybe we can help bring it to birth both in them and in ourselves.

Be kind to this nation of ours by remembering that New Haven, New Hope, Shalom, are the names not just of our oldest towns but of our holiest dreams which most of the time are threatened by the madness of no enemy without as dangerously as they are threatened by our own madness within.

"You have tasted of the kindness of the Lord," Peter wrote in his letter, and ultimately that, of course, is the kindness, the holiness, the sainthood and sanity, we are all of us called to. So that by God's grace we may "grow up to salvation" at last.

The way the light falls through the windows. The sounds our silence makes when we come together like this. The sense we have of each other's presence. The feeling in the air that one way or another we are all of us here to give each other our love, and to give God our love. This kind moment itself is a door that holiness enters through. May it enter you. May it enter me. To the world's saving.

13

The Church

*And he called to him his twelve disciples and gave them
authority over unclean spirits, to cast them out, and to heal
every disease and every infirmity. The names of the twelve
apostles are these: first, Simon, who is called Peter, and
Andrew his brother; James the son of Zebedee, and John his
brother; Philip and Bartholomew; Thomas and Matthew the
tax collector; James the son of Alphaeus, and Thaddeus;
Simon the Canaanean and Judas Iscariot, who betrayed him.
These twelve Jesus sent out, charging them, "Go nowhere
among the Gentiles, and enter no town of the Samaritans,
but go rather to the lost sheep of the house of Israel. And
preach as you go, saying, "The kingdom of heaven is at
hand." Heal the sick, raise the dead, cleanse lepers, cast out
demons.* —Matthew 10:1–8

I suppose the most famous of the twelve disciples was
Simon Peter, who was the one who seems to have been the
first to realize who Jesus actually was. He was also the one
who occasioned the only pun Jesus is on record as having
made when he said that Peter, whose name means rock in
Greek, was the rock he was going to found his Church on.
There was also Peter's brother Andrew, and Zebedee's two

sons, James and John, plus another James and another Simon known as the Canaanean. Thaddeus and Bartholomew were among them too, whoever they were, and Matthew the tax collector and Philip, who was from Peter's home town of Bethsaida and Thomas the doubter and finally Judas Iscariot, of course, who in the garden, by moonlight, betrayed his friend by kissing him and was thus the last human being to touch him except for the purpose of inflicting pain.

Those were the people Jesus started his Church with as Matthew names them anyway. We know so little about them and would give so much to know more. If they weren't all of them Jews, presumably most of them were. They've had a pretty bad press over the centuries, and by and large they seem to have deserved it. On the night of the arrest, for instance, not one of them apparently so much as raised a finger to defend their friend except Peter, who cut the ear off one of the High Priest's slaves with his sword which can hardly have made matters anything but worse and might have led to worse still if Jesus hadn't told him in effect to cool it, adding that those who live by the sword usually end up dying by the sword, which is a point so close to the heart of his message in general that you'd think they'd have gotten it by then.

But of course the other reason for their bad press is that they never seem to have gotten *any* of his points very well, or if and when they did get them, never seem to have lived by them very well, which makes them people very much like you, if I may say so, and also, if I may say so, very much like me. That is to say they were *human beings*. Jesus made his Church out of human beings with more or less the same mixture in them of cowardice and guts, of intelligence and stupidity, of selfishness and generosity, of openness of heart and sheer cussedness as you would be apt to find in any of us. The reason he made his Church out of human beings is that human beings were all there was to make it out of. In fact as far as I know, human beings are all there is to make it out of still. It's a point worth remembering.

It is also a point worth remembering that even after Jesus made these human beings into a Church, they seem to have gone right on being human beings. They actually knew Jesus as their friend. They sat at his feet and listened to him speak; they ate with him and tramped the countryside with him; they witnessed his miracles; but not even all of that turned them into heroes. They kept on being as human as they'd always been with most of the same strengths and most of the same weaknesses.

And finally when it comes to remembering things, we do well to keep in mind that the idea of becoming the Church wasn't their idea. It was Jesus' idea. It was Jesus who made them a Church. They didn't come together the way like-minded people come together to make a club. They didn't come together the way a group of men might come together to form a baseball team or the way a group of women might come together to lobby for higher teachers' salaries. They came together because Jesus called them to come together. That is what the Greek word *ekklēsia* means from which we get our word church. It means those who have been *called out of* the way the original twelve were called out of fishing or tax collecting or running a kosher restaurant or a laundromat or whatever else they happened to be involved in at the time.

Somebody appears on your front stoop speaking your name, say, and you go down to open the door to see what's up. Sometimes while it's still raining, the sun comes out from behind the clouds, and suddenly, arching against the gray sky, there is a rainbow which people stop doing whatever they're doing to look at. They lay down their fishing nets, their tax forms, their bridge hands, their golf clubs or newspapers, to gaze at the sky because what is happening up there is so marvelous they can't help themselves. Something like that, I think, is the way those twelve men Matthew names were called to become a church, plus Mary, Martha, Joanna, and all the other women and men who one way or another became part of it too. One way or another Christ called them. That's how it happened. They saw the marvel of him arch across the grayness of things—the grayness of their own lives perhaps, of life itself. They heard his voice calling their names. And they went.

They seem to have gone right on working at pretty much whatever they'd been working at before which means that he didn't so much call them out of their ordinary lives as he called them out of believing that ordinary life is ordinary. He called them to see that no matter how ordinary it may seem to us as we live it, life is extraordinary. "The Kingdom of God is at hand" is the way he put it to them, and the way he told them to put it to others. Life even at its most monotonous and backbreaking and heart-numbing has the Kingdom buried in it the way a field has treasure buried in it, he said. The Kingdom of God is as close to us as some precious keepsake we've been looking for for years which is lying just in the next room under the rug all but crying out to us to come find it. If we only had eyes to see and ears to hear and wits to understand, we would know that the Kingdom of God in the sense of holiness, goodness, beauty is as close as breathing and is crying out to be born both within ourselves and within the world; we would know that the Kingdom of God is what we all of us hunger for above all other things even when we don't know its name or realize that it's what we're starving to death for. The Kingdom of God is where our best dreams come from and our truest prayers. We glimpse it at those moments when we find ourselves being better than we are and wiser than we know. We catch sight of it when at some moment of crisis a strength seems to come to us that is greater than our own strength. The Kingdom of God is where we belong. It is home, and whether we realize it or not, I think we are all of us homesick for it.

A fat man drives by in his Chevy pickup with a cigarette in his mouth and on his rear bumper a sticker that says *Jesus Loves You*. There's a shotgun slung across the back window. He is not a stranger we've never seen before and couldn't care less if we ever see again. He is our brother, our father. He is our son. It is true that we have never seen him before, and that we will probably never see him again—just that one quick glimpse as he goes by at twenty-five miles an hour because it is a school zone—but if we can somehow fully realize the truth of that, fully understand that this is the one and only time we will ever see him, we will treasure that one and only time the way we treasure the rainbow in the sky or the ring we finally found under the rug after years of looking for it. The old woman with thick glasses who sits in front of us at the movies eating popcorn is our mother, our sister, our child grown old, and once we know that, once we see her for who she truly is, everything about her becomes precious—the skinny back of her neck, the way she puts her hand over her mouth when she laughs.

These are not ordinary people any more than life is ordinary. They are extraordinary people. Life is extraordinary, and the extraordinariness of it is what Jesus calls the Kingdom of God. The extraordinariness of it is that in the Kingdom of God we all belong to each other the way families do. We are all of us brothers and sisters in it. We are all of us mothers and fathers and children of each other in it because that is what we are called together as the Church to be. That is what being the Church means. We are called by God to love each other the way Jesus says that God has loved us. That is the Good News about God—the Gospel—which he came to proclaim. Loving each other and loving God and being loved by God is what the Kingdom is. No scientific truth or philosophic truth, no truth of art or music or literature, is as important as that Kingdom truth.

Loving God means rejoicing in him. It means trusting him when you can think of a hundred reasons not to trust anything. It means praying to him even when you don't feel like it. It means watching for him in the beauty and sadness and gladness and mystery of your own life and of life around you. Loving each other doesn't mean loving each other in some sentimental, unrealistic, greeting-card kind of way but the way families love each other even though they may fight tooth and nail and get fed to the teeth with each other and drive each other crazy yet all the time know deep down in their hearts that they belong to each other and need each other and can't imagine what life would be without each other—even the ones they often wish had never been born.

Matthew the tax collector and Thomas the doubter. Peter the rock and Judas the traitor. Mary Magdalene and Lazarus' sister Martha. And the popcorn-eating old woman.

And the fat man in the pickup. They are all our family, and you and I are their family and each other's family, because that is what Jesus has called us as the Church to be. Our happiness is all mixed up with each other's happiness and our peace with each other's peace. Our own happiness, our own peace, can never be complete until we find some way of sharing it with people who the way things are now have no happiness and know no peace. Jesus calls us to show this truth forth, live this truth forth. Be the light of the world, he says. Where there are dark places, be the light especially there. Be the salt of the earth. Bring out the true flavor of what it is to be alive truly. Be truly alive. Be life-givers to others. That is what Jesus tells the disciples to be. That is what Jesus tells his Church, tells us, to be and do. Love each other. Heal the sick, he says. Raise the dead. Cleanse lepers. Cast out demons. That is what loving each other means. If the Church is doing things like that, then it is being what Jesus told it to be. If it is not doing things like that—no matter how many other good and useful things it may be doing instead—then it is not being what Jesus told it to be. It is as simple as that.

The old woman has gone to the movies to help take her mind off the fact that she has cancer. Cancer is a sickness that you and I don't know how to heal, more's the pity, but it is not her only sickness. Her other sickness is being lonely and scared, and in some ways that sickness is the worse of the two. Sometimes she wakes up in the middle of the night and thinks about it—wishes she had somebody she could talk to about it or just somebody she could go to the movies with once in a while and share her popcorn with. Heal her, Jesus says.

The fat man in the pickup has a son who is dying. He is dying of AIDS. It was his wife who put the Jesus Loves You sticker on his bumper. The way he sees it, if you do not believe in God any more, it doesn't make much difference whether Jesus loves you or not. If God lets things happen to people like what has happened to his son, then what is the point of believing in God. Raise him, Jesus says.

"Heal the sick, raise the dead, cleanse lepers, cast out demons," Jesus tells the disciples. That is the work he sets us. In other words, we are to be above all else healers, and that means of course that we are also to be healed because God knows you and I are in as much need of healing as anybody else, and being healed and healing go hand in hand. God knows we have our own demons to be cast out, our own uncleanness to be cleansed. Neurotic anxiety happens to be my own particular demon, a floating sense of doom that has ruined many of what could have been, should have been, the happiest days of my life, and more than a few times in my life I have been raised from such ruins, which is another way of saying that more than a few times in my life I have been raised from death—death of the spirit anyway, death of the heart—by the healing power that Jesus calls us both to heal with and to be healed by.

I remember an especially dark time of my life. One of my children was sick, and in my anxiety for her I was in my own way as sick as she was. Then one day the phone rang, and it was a man named Lou Patrick, whom I didn't know very well then though he has become a great friend since, a minister from Charlotte, North Carolina, which is about eight hundred miles or so from Rupert, Vermont, where I live. I assumed he was calling from home and asked him how things were going down there only to hear him say that, no, he wasn't in Charlotte. He was at an inn about twenty minutes away from my house in Rupert. He knew something about what was going on in my family and in me, and he said he thought maybe it would be some help to have an extra friend around for a day or two. The reason he didn't tell me in advance that he was coming was that he knew I would tell him for Heaven's sake not to do anything so crazy, so for Heaven's sake he did something crazier still which was to come those eight hundred miles without telling me he was coming so that for all he knew I might not even have been there. But as luck had it, I was there, and for a day or two he was there with me. He was there for me. I don't think anything we found to say to each other amounted to very much. There was nothing particularly religious about it. I don't remember even spending much time talking about my troubles with him. We just took a couple of walks, had a meal or two together and smoked our pipes. I drove him around to see some of the countryside, and that was about it.

I have never forgotten how he came all that distance just for that, and I'm sure he has never forgotten it either. I also believe that although as far as I can remember we never so much as mentioned the name of Christ, Christ was as much in the air we breathed those few days as the fragrance of our pipes was in the air, or the dappled light of the woods we walked through. I believe that for a little time we both of us touched the hem of Christ's garment. I know that for a little time we both of us were healed.

We are called to be Christs to each other like that, I think. Like Peter, like Thomas, the Marys, Joanna, we are called to be not just human beings but human beings open to the possibility of being transformed by the grace of God as it comes to us who knows how or when—in the fragrance of pipe smoke in the air, the band of a rainbow arched against the gray sky. Somebody calling on the phone: "Just twenty minutes down the road did you say? Good God, you must be crazy!" And that is just it, of course. We are called to be crazy exactly like that. We are called by the good God to be the hands and feet and heart of Christ to each other.

The church buildings and budgets came later. The forms of church government, the priests and pastors, Baptists and Protestants. The Sunday services with everybody in their best clothes, the Sunday Schools and choirs all came later. So did the Bible study groups and the rummage sales. So did the preachers, the ones on TV who make you sick to your stomach with their phoniness and vulgarity and the ones closer to home who so often, when I listen to them, seem to proclaim a faith that rarely seems to have much to do either with their own real day-to-day lives in this world or with mine, and the ones also through whose words every once in a while the Word itself touches your heart. They all came later. Maybe the best thing that could happen to the church would be for some great tidal wave of history to wash all that away—the church buildings tumbling, the church money all lost, the church bulletins blowing through the air like dead leaves, the differences between preachers and congregations all lost too. Then all we would have left would be each other and Christ, which was all there was in the first place.

"Truly I say to you, as you did it to the least of these my brethren, you did it to me," Jesus said, which means that in this world now Jesus *is* each other. Heal the sick and be healed. Raise the dead and be raised. Everything that matters comes out of doing those things. Doing those things is what the Church is, and when it doesn't do those things, it doesn't matter much what else it does. Preach as you go, saying "The kingdom of Heaven is at hand," Jesus told the disciples. *Be* the Kingdom of Heaven.

The Kingdom of Heaven is only twenty minutes down the road, for Christ's sake. The Kingdom of Heaven is in the movie theater as the old woman gets up to leave, shaking popcorn crumbs out of her lap. The Kingdom of Heaven is there as the fat man goes driving by in his pickup with the bumper sticker he can't believe in. The Kingdom of Heaven is in the eyes of love and longing and blessing that we raise to look at him as though he was a rainbow in the sky.

14

The Kingdom of God

*The beginning of the Gospel of Jesus Christ, the Son of God.
As it is written in Isaiah the prophet,
"Behold, I send my messenger before thy face, who shall
prepare thy way; the voice of one crying in the wilderness:
Prepare the way of the Lord, make his paths straight—"
John the baptizer appeared in the wilderness preaching a
baptism of repentance for the forgiveness of sins. And there
went out to him all the country of Judea, and they all were
baptized by him in the river Jordan, confessing their sins.
Now John was clothed with camel's hair, and had a leather
girdle around his waist, and ate locusts and wild honey. And
he preached, saying, "After me comes he who is mightier than
I, the thong of whose sandals I am not worthy to stoop down
and untie. I have baptized you with water; but he will baptize you with the Holy Spirit." In those days Jesus came from
Nazareth of Galilee and was baptized by John in the Jordan.
And when he came up out of the water, immediately he saw
the heavens opened and the Spirit descending upon him like a
dove; and a voice came from heaven, "Thou art my beloved
Son; with thee I am well pleased." The Spirit immediately
drove him out into the wilderness. And he was in the wilderness forty days, tempted by Satan; and he was with the wild
beasts; and the angels ministered to him. Now after John was
arrested, Jesus came into Galilee, preaching the gospel of God,*

*and saying, "The time is fulfilled, and the kingdom of God is
at hand; repent, and believe in the gospel."*
                                        —Mark 1:1–15

I always get the feeling as I read the opening verses of the
Gospel of Mark that he is in a terrible rush, that he can't
wait to reach the place where he feels the Gospel really
begins. He says absolutely nothing about how Jesus was
born. He gets through the baptism in no time flat. He barely
mentions the temptation in the wilderness. And only then,
after racing through those first fourteen verses, does he get
where he seems to have been racing to—the real beginning
as he sees it—and that is the opening words of Jesus himself. Up to that point it has all gone so fast that hardly anybody except John the Baptist knows who Jesus really is yet,
just as it might be said that most of the time hardly any of
us knows who Jesus really is yet either.

He is destined to have a greater impact on the next two
thousand years of human history than anybody else in history—we know that now—but here at the beginning of Mark
nobody knows it yet. Not a single syllable has escaped his
lips yet, as Mark tells it. The ant lays down her crumb to listen. The very stars in the sky hold their breath. Nobody in
the world knows what Jesus is going to say yet, and maybe
it's worthwhile pretending we don't know either—pretending we've never heard him yet ourselves which may be closer
to the truth than we think.

"The time is fulfilled," he says. "And the kingdom of
God is at hand. Repent and believe in the gospel." That is
how he launches the Gospel—his first recorded words. There

is a kind of breathlessness in those three short, urgent sentences. The question is, what do they urgently mean to us who know them so well that we hardly hear them any more? If they mean anything to us at all, urgent or otherwise, what in God's name is it?

At least there is no great mystery about what "the time is fulfilled" means, I think. "The time is fulfilled" means the time is up. That is the dark side of it anyway, saving the bright side of it till later. It means that it is possible we are living in the last days. There was a time when you could laugh that kind of message off if you saw some bearded crazy parading through the city streets with it painted on a sandwich board, but you have to be crazy yourself to laugh at it in our nuclear age. What with *glasnost* and *perestroika* and what seems to be the gradual break-up of world communism, things look more hopeful than they have for a long time, but the world is still a powder keg. The missiles are still in their silos, the vast armies are still under arms. And there are other dangers potentially more dangerous now than even nuclear war. There is AIDS. There is terrorism. There are drugs and more to the point the darkness of our time that makes people seek escape in drugs. There is the slow poisoning of what we call "the environment" of all things, as if with that antiseptic term we can conceal from ourselves that what we are really poisoning is home, is here, is us.

It is no wonder that the books and newspapers we read, the movies and TV we watch, are obsessed with the dark and demonic, are full of death and violence. It is as if the reason we wallow in them is that they help us keep our minds off the real death, the real violence. And God knows the Church of

Christ has its darkness and demons too. On television and in cults it is so discredited by religious crooks and phonies and vaudevillians, and in thousands of respectable pulpits it is so bland and banal and without passion, that you wonder sometimes not only if it will survive but if it even deserves to survive. As a character in Woody Allen's *Hannah and Her Sisters* puts it, "If Jesus came back and saw what was going on in his name, he'd never stop throwing up."

In other words, a lot of the kinds of things that happen at the ends of civilizations are happening today in our civilization, and there are moments when it is hard to avoid feeling not only that our time is up but that it is high time for our time to be up. That we're ready to fall from the branch like overripe fruit under the weight of our own decay. Something like that, I think, is the shadow side of what Jesus means when he says that the time is fulfilled.

If he meant that the world was literally coming to an end back there in the first century A.D., then insofar as he was a human, he was humanly wrong. But if he meant that the world is always coming to an end, if he meant that we carry within us the seeds of our own destruction no less than the Roman and Jewish worlds of his day carried it within them, if he meant that in the long run we are always in danger of one way or another destroying ourselves utterly, then of course he was absolutely right.

But Jesus says something else too. Thank God for that. He says our time is up, but he also says that the Kingdom of God is at hand. The Kingdom of God is so close we can almost reach out our hands and touch it. It is so close that sometimes it almost reaches out and takes us by the hand. The Kingdom of God, that is. Not man's kingdom. Not

Saddam Hussein's kingdom, not Bush's kingdom, not Gorbachev's kingdom. Not any of the kingdoms that still have nuclear missiles aimed at each other's heads, that worry like us about counting calories while hundreds of thousands starve to death. But God's Kingdom. Jesus says it is the Kingdom of God that is at hand. If anybody else said it, we would hoot him off the stage. But it is Jesus who says it. Even people who don't believe in him can't quite hoot him off the stage. Even people who have long since written him off can't help listening to him.

The Kingdom of God? Time after time Jesus tries to drum into our heads what he means by it. He heaps parable upon parable like a madman. He tries shouting it. He tries whispering it. The Kingdom of God is like a treasure, like a pearl, like a seed buried in the ground. It is like a great feast that everybody is invited to and nobody wants to attend.

What he seems to be saying is that the Kingdom of God is the time, or a time beyond time, when it will no longer be humans in their lunacy who are in charge of the world but God in his mercy who will be in charge of the world. It's the time above all else for wild rejoicing—like getting out of jail, like being cured of cancer, like finally, at long last, coming home. And it is at hand, Jesus says.

Can we take such a message seriously, knowing all that we know and having seen all that we've seen? Can we take it any more seriously than the Land of Oz? It's not so hard to believe in a day of wrath and a last judgment—just read the newspapers—but is the Kingdom of God any more than a good dream? Has anybody ever seen it—if not the full glory of it than at least a glimpse of it off in the shimmering distance somewhere?

It was a couple of springs ago. I was driving into New York City from New Jersey on one of those crowded, fast-moving turnpikes you enter it by. It was very warm. There was brilliant sunshine, and the cars glittered in it as they went tearing by. The sky was cloudless and blue. Around Newark a huge silver plane traveling in the same direction as I was made its descent in a slow diagonal and touched down soft as a bird on the airstrip just a few hundred yards away from me as I went driving by. I had music on the radio, but I didn't need it. The day made its own music—the hot spring sun and the hum of the road, the roar of the great trucks passing and of my own engine, the hum of my own thoughts. When I came out of the Lincoln Tunnel, the city was snarled and seething with traffic as usual; but at the same time there was some-thing about it that was not usual.

It was gorgeous traffic, it was beautiful traffic—that's what was not usual. It was a beauty to see, to hear, to smell, even to be part of. It was so dazzlingly alive it all but took my breath away. It rattled and honked and chattered with life—the people, the colors of their clothes, the marvelous hodgepodge of their faces, all of it; the taxis, the shops, the blinding sidewalks. The spring day made everybody a celebri-ty—blacks, whites, Hispanics, every last one of them. It made even the litter and clamor and turmoil of it a kind of miracle.

There was construction going on as I inched my way east along 54th street, and some wino, some bum, was stretched out on his back in the sun on a pile of lumber as if it was an alpine meadow he was stretched out on and he was made of money. From the garage where I left the car, I continued my way on foot. In the high-ceilinged public atrium on the ground floor of a large office building there were people on benches eating their sandwiches. Some of them were dressed to kill. Some of them were in jeans and sneakers. There were young ones and old ones. Daylight was flooding in on them, and there were green plants growing and a sense of deep peace as they ate their lunches mostly in silence. A big man in a clown costume and whiteface took out a tubular yellow balloon big around as a noodle, blew it up and twisted it squeakily into a dove of peace which he handed to the bug-eyed child watching him. I am not making this up. It all happened.

In some ways it was like a dream and in other ways as if I had woken up from a dream. I had the feeling that I had never seen the city so *real* before in all my life. I was walking along Central Park South near Columbus Circle at the foot of the park when a middle-aged black woman came toward me going the other way. Just as she passed me, she spoke. What she said was, "Jesus loves you." That is what she said: "Jesus loves you," just like that. She said it in as everyday a voice as if she had been saying good morning, and I was so caught off guard that it wasn't till she was lost in the crowd that I realized what she had said and wondered if I could possibly ever find her again and thank her, if I could ever catch up with her and say, "Yes. If I believe anything worth believing in this whole world, I believe that. He loves me. He loves you. He loves the whole doomed, damned pack of us."

For the rest of the way I was going, the streets I walked on were paved with gold. Nothing was different. Everything was different. The city was transfigured. I was transfigured. It was a new New York coming down out of heaven adorned like a bride prepared for her husband. "The dwelling of God is with men. He will dwell with them, and they shall be his people ... he will wipe away every tear from their eyes, and death shall be no more, neither shall there be any mourning, nor crying, nor pain any more, for the former things have passed away." That is the city that for a moment I saw.

For a moment it was not the world as it *is* that I saw but the world as it *might be,* as something deep within the world wants to be and is preparing to be, the way in darkness a seed prepares for growth, the way leaven works in bread.

Buried beneath the surface of all the dirt and noise and crime and poverty and pollution of that terrifying city, I glimpsed the treasure that waits to make it a holy city—a city where human beings dwell in love and peace with each other and with God and where the only tears there are are tears of joy and reunion. Jesus said that as soon as the fig tree "becomes tender and puts forth its leaves, you know summer is near. So also, when you see these things taking place, you know that [the Son of man] is near, at the very gates." For a few very brief and enormously moving minutes that day, the city itself became tender, put out leaves, and I knew beyond all doubt that more than summer was near, that something extraordinary was at the gates, something extraordinary was at least at the gates inside me. "The kingdom of God is within you—or 'among you,'—" Jesus said, and for a little while it was so.

All over the world you can hear it stirring if you stop to listen, I think. Good things are happening in and through all sorts of people. They don't speak with a single voice, these people. No one person has emerged yet as their leader. They are divided into many groups pulling in many different directions. Some are pressing for an end to the nuclear arms race. Some are pressing for women's rights, some for civil rights, or gay rights, or human rights. Some are concerned primarily with world hunger or with the way we are little by little destroying the oceans, the rain forests, the air we breathe. There are lots of different people saying lots of different things and some of them put us off with their craziness and there are lots of points to argue with them about, but at their best they seem to be acting out of a single profound impulse, which is best described with words like: Tolerance. Compassion. Sanity. Hope. Justice. It is an impulse that has always been part of the human heart, but it seems to be welling up into the world with new power in our age now even as the forces of darkness are welling up with new power in our age now too. That is the bright side, I think, the glad and hopeful side, of what Jesus means by "The time is fulfilled." He means the time is ripe.

Humanly speaking, if we have any chance to survive, I suspect that it is men and women who act out of that deep impulse who are our chance. By no means will they themselves bring about the Kingdom of God. It is God alone who brings about his Kingdom. Even with the best will in the world and out of our noblest impulses, we can't do that. But there is something that we can do and must do, Jesus says, and that is *repent*. Biblically speaking, to repent doesn't mean to feel sorry about, to regret. It means to turn, to turn around 180 degrees. It means to undergo a complete change of mind, heart, direction. To individuals and to nations both, Jesus says the same thing. Turn *away from* madness, cruelty, shallowness, blindness. Turn *toward* that tolerance, compassion, sanity, hope, justice which we all have in us at our best.

We cannot make the Kingdom of God happen, but we can put out leaves as it draws near. We can be kind to each other. We can be kind to ourselves. We can drive back the darkness a little. We can make green places within ourselves and among ourselves where God can make his Kingdom happen. That transfigured city. Those people of every color, class, condition, eating their sandwiches together in that quiet place. The clown and the child. The sunlight that made everybody in those teeming streets a superstar. The bum napping like a millionaire on his pile of two-by-fours. The beautiful traffic surging all around me and the beautiful things that I could feel surging inside myself, in that holy place which is inside all of us. Turn *that* way. Everybody. While there is still time. Pray for the Kingdom. Watch for signs of it. Live as though it is here already because there are moments when it almost is, such as those moments in Tiananmen Square before the massacre started when the students were gentle and the soldiers were gentle and something so holy and human was trying to happen there that it was hard to see pictures of it without having tears come to your eyes.

And "Believe in the gospel." That's the last of those first words that Jesus speaks. Believe in the good news. Believe in what that black woman said. Hurrying along Central Park South, she didn't even stop as she said it. It was as if she didn't have time to stop. She said it on the run the way Mark's gospel says it. "Jesus loves you," she said. It was a corny thing for her to say, of course. Embarrassing. A screwball thing to blurt out to a total stranger on a crowded sidewalk. But, "Jesus loves you." She said it anyway. And that *is* the good news of the gospel, exactly that.

The power which is in Jesus, and before which all other powers on earth and in Heaven give way, the power that holds all things in existence from the sparrow's eye to the farthest star, is above all else a loving power. That means we are loved even in our lostness. That means we are precious, every one of us, even as we pass on the street without so much as noticing each other's faces. Every city is precious. The world is precious. Someday the precious time will be up for each of us. But the Kingdom of God is at hand. Nothing is different and everything is different. It reaches out to each of our precious hands while there's still time.

Repent and believe in the gospel, Jesus says. Turn around and believe that the good news that we are loved is gooder than we ever dared hope, and that to believe in that good news, to live out of it and toward it, to be in love with that good news, is of all glad things in this world the gladdest thing of all.

Amen, and come, Lord Jesus.